STUFF IT!

AdVANture Time!

A campervan tour around England and Scotland

By

Ruby Allure

For Tamsin, Marie and Kerry

Without you I would not have written this...

CHAPTER 1

THE TRIGGER

Hello Ruby, I understand that you are the woman my husband is currently having an affair with.

I re-read the text from an unknown number. I then read the next message.

You may not be aware but Ryan and I are still married. We are and will continue to be married. We have been married for seventeen years and committed to 'until death us do part'. I suggest you take the opportunity to leave while you can.

Whoever had written that knew my name and the name of the chap I was dating. Also she, if it was a she, had discovered my phone number or had purposely extracted it from somewhere.

I didn't respond, I was too busy at work and I didn't have the headspace to react. Instead, I intended to watch.

The next day another text onslaught arrived.

My husband has just left our marital home. He said to you that he was up in Scotland to look after the children. That is somewhat true. What he hasn't told you is that he and I still sleep together. I know he is on his way to see you because I have been reading your texts. He really has been telling you a lot of lies. Yes he is in the Navy, he is not divorced, not even separated. Also it isn't just you that he is seeing. He is on a whole number of dating apps and appears to be shagging numerous women all around the country.

I did not respond. You can't negotiate with crazy; plus, I thought I would let whoever was contacting me play itself out. If she was married to Ryan, and he was having numerous affairs, then why would she stay and endure such circumstances for seventeen years? Why would she continue to sleep with him? Admittedly he was bloody good at sausage hiding, but was that enough reason to remain married to a man who was quite likely to be fertilising many female fields? An unsettled feeling resonated through my stomach. It felt like the beginning of the end. I turned my attention to work and looked forward to spending Friday evening arranging 'stuff' in Blossom, my campervan.

You would not believe how many women he has contacted. He seems to have a type – like you. He likes the fair hair, the blue eyes and women into fitness. Well that is the current trend anyway.

Another text.

He just kissed me goodbye and got on the train. Here is a selfie of us kissing. You see, I am still married to him, if you don't believe me.

You can only avoid this for a certain amount of time. I skimmed the image for dates and times and enhanced the image. There was nothing additional to reveal the time other than the train time, which corresponded to the departure time. The thing is Ryan followed timing cycles, he was a creature of routine. The train from

Glasgow to Southampton left at certain times and Ryan would follow those timings every time he travelled back and forth. I checked the photo properties, I could only identify when the image was sent, rather than when it was taken. Admittedly I could remote access her phone, skim her photo-library and determine her identity. Although, I would only abuse my skills and my work by doing that. One can easily become obsessive and infiltrate people's lives through their phones and through the 'back-door technology'. One couldn't spend one's life delving into dates' pasts because no matter what you did, you would always find something. Pretty much everyone had had a dirty patch on their doorstep while many had created a definitive doorstep dung-pile.

Ryan was due to arrive late that evening for the weekend. I would watch for details and nuances in his behaviour. The woman's texts were growing desperate.

I can see you are naïve and desperate to be with my husband. He is a compulsive liar and you have bought into the lies. He has lied to you and just wants to use you for sex.

She was ruining my peace so I blocked her. So much for simply watching. I also intended to spend my evening enjoying van-space until he arrived.

Ryan text me telling me how excited he was about the weekend. That he had been so bored in Scotland. He had had a nice time with his boys but ended up doing all the 'jobs' around the house that his ex-wife had left for him. I asked him what time he would arrive – it was usually around ten-ish, so we wouldn't go out for dinner, not that he could afford to anyway. I then read the 'wife's texts once more.

Ryan and I had met on a dating app, he was warm, fun and lively. From the moment we met he was affectionate, playful and up for adventure. We also had an intense chemistry which ignited within the first few dates and after the first kiss. Passion stampeded through our veins and our bodies were like magnets. It made such a change from some of the dull dates I had experienced. Maybe that was why I was in avoidance.

According to Ryan he split up with his wife and moved to Plymouth because he was in the navy. He was then transferred to Portsmouth where he became land-based. He was originally from Polynesia and looked like a Maori rugby player. He had a huge smile, kind eyes and an atmosphere that felt like a warm warrior. He was attentive, made an effort, smelled nice, didn't snore, was tidy, and was on time. When he said he would call he did. After my other dating experiences Ryan came across like a golden nugget. He said what he wanted and had excellent communication skills. He also listened when I spoke and heard what I said. Should that have provided any cause for alarm? No. With the new relationship, summer was in full force. I lived by the beach and worked building technology. I was scoping out a campervan when we first met and Blossom was delivered the week when Ryan and I had been together six months – an ani-vani-versary. I was so excited by the prospect of Ryan and I adventuring together. The future, 'pre-affair-accusing texts', looked amazing. The week Blossom arrived was the same week the texts were sent. The thing is I was a technology-building analyst, my mind noticed details and admittedly I had trust issues. Numerous exes had turned out to have dark pasts, or shady dealings. I hoped that I had moved beyond that. I found it odd how someone (moi) who was honest, kept attracting misconstruers of truth. Maybe Ryan was part of the same pattern.

At ten o'clock I stood outside the train station. That huge smile, the caramel skin and the green eyes greeted me. He swept me up, spun me around and then cuddled me. He held me and whispered, 'Can we just stay here a while. I have missed you so much'. He sniffed my hair, he sniffed my neck and then buried his head into the nape. He just rested and breathed. 'My God I love you,' he whispered. 'My God I am so lucky to have you. I have missed you.'

In the back of my mind the texts repeated in cycles.

CHAPTER 2

A LITTLE CRAZY?

So I had this crazy thought... Well, I might have had a few actually. However, one thought will create a thought stream, which becomes a thought river and can eventually become a vast thought ocean. That one thought was one of those little intuitive voices which whispers. I am often too busy to hear because I have tick lists to tick, things to get done and work to deliver. That little voice whispered again and again - I kind of heard it but ignored it due to time limitation. Sound familiar? Well that little voice generally cuts you some slack until it says 'Right you are going to listen, and that means you have to stop!' My friend has an analogy: poked by a toothpick, a prod from the chopstick then a smack around the face with a five foot plank. Well that plank, mowed me down and laid me down with a rather intense virus, which forced me to take time off work. The infallible, health obsessed, work tank had to lay in bed and do nothing for close to a week. What made it worse was my work space was just a few rooms away... It beckoned me, yet the little voice had other plans... It intended to make me listen.

Pouring with sweat and coughing up a lung isn't fun, especially when you are so conditioned to be 'doing'. Stopping and recuperating feels like failure. The drive to deliver over-rides any sense of wellbeing. To be productive and work, work, work because everything is urgent, urgent, super urgent and urgent, urgent, URGENT!!! had become the new normal.

Ridiculous eh? Since when had the world become like that? Well, it became like that because it is based in fear. It takes your body, kicking your legs from beneath you, to sit on your arse. In that moment of stopping you realise how caught up in the bullshit you have become. It is then the epiphanies begin. You realise how stressed and exhausted you have been. There was no space to digest and process life because there was another project and a deadline. I had become a human mental sausage resource. I realised I lived on coffee and adrenaline because there was another project, a deadline and a bill to pay…

So what was the crazy thought?

What if life didn't have to be like this?

EEEEEEEEEEEEEEEEEEEEEEEk! Went something within me and tried to shut it down.

What if life could be bliss and not stress?

What if life could flow and be easy and not a struggle?

What if I could be free to do what I want whenever I want with whoever I want?

See… f*ing crazy!

Then the thoughts spiralled. That little voice climbed onto a podium and began a rather indulgent monologue.

What if you could be at peace?

What if you could rest?

What if you could live a life filled with joy?

What if you didn't just work all of the time?

I was a sitting duck for an onslaught of thoughts. I should have known they were brewing too. Work had been intense, I was reaching my upper mental capacity on a daily basis. I was doing yoga twice a day and - making sure I exercised the tension out of my system, yet the constant feeling of 'being on edge' remained.

I wondered whether my rather unexpected purchase of a campervan had fuelled the thoughts. My logic had been that I wanted to be able to work at different locations. That was just before the 'plague' hit. The funny thing is I had agreed to go camping with some friends who thought it would be a laugh for women in their mid-forties to hang out in tents in a field (campsite). It was great fun around the campfire gazing up at the stars until it came to an unfortunate night of tent-trauma. The neighbours sounded like mating walruses. A bloke called Darryl snored and farted all night. He even managed a half-tune from his anus. As a final finale some drunk tripped over one of my guide ropes and landed on my tent. Luckily that person landed on the opposite side of my double blow-up mattress and launched me in the air. Have you ever woken from a half-slumber levitating? Now that is quite a strange state of affairs and makes flying dreams more realistic.

Once the embarrassed drunk scrambled away in the darkness I laid thinking. I had always wanted a campervan but had always found reasons why I shouldn't. There was the fact it would be a large item to drive. Reversing - my God the thought of that. In addition my skills at parking weren't the best. Numerous times people had pointed at my car and laughed at the angle and distance from the curb. One of my exes said it looked more abandoned than parked. I called it expressive parking – I never got away with it. Being launched in the air at night by an anonymous drunk was a turning point for me. The funny thing was a couple of my friends had sleepless nights too. At lunchtime, when most of them emerged from their tents, we discussed vans because only one of us had had a delightful night's sleep. She had been tucked up in a van with a fixed bed, shower and toilet. When I returned home that evening, I made an appointment with a van dealer. I had been scoping out my different options and two of my friends had the type I liked and they loved them.

There was one van on the website that was already built and fitted my specifications. However, when I viewed the gold exterior with red and black interior it reminded me of a weird pervert's palace. I admit I was disappointed, and sighed. I then noticed my new van which became 'Blossom'. She was an elegant silver van who had just arrived from Japan. She had 22,000 miles on the clock. She wasn't converted yet which meant I could choose my interior. I had a look at the other examples in the showroom and said 'Can I have that interior put in her?' The answer was yes and that was it. Three months later Blossom was delivered all fitted out. I had heating, solar panels and an awning added. It was easy... You know how we blow these things out of proportion – well it need not be the case.

The next big challenge was to drive her. Can you believe it - she was easier to drive and park than my car. What's more, I had exchanged my car for the van and was terrified I had made a huge mistake. Oh no... Not at all. Being high up in the van meant I could see much better. The mirrors were brilliant and I had a reverse parking camera. Everything I had been concerned about had been taken care of. Worrying was a waste of time because we adapt and learn when new circumstances unfold. So all in all Blossom was a blessing and one that arrived with ease and flow.

CHAPTER 3

THE NAMING

Isn't it funny how we name inanimate objects? Well since Blossom was from Japan, and one of my most amazing travels took me to the Sakura festival, I was going to name her Sakura. It was a beautiful name in honour of her Japanese origin and the beautiful memories I had of that travel adventure. The thing was Blossom stuck because I kept having to explain what Sakura meant. When I told my Japanese friends that I had imported my van, they were thrilled. I told them I had named her Blossom to remind me of my wonderful trip with them. A week later some blossom bumper stickers arrived in the post. That evening Blossom's bottom bloomed with a beautiful picture sticker with a floral arrangement in pink. She felt complete.

I told Ryan about my bumper stickers and he was less thrilled. 'That makes it a girl's van.' Well it was a girl's van, it was my van, not 'our' van. I had worked and saved the money... to have MY van. He didn't even have a car. He said it was because he lived in Portsmouth and didn't need one because everything was accessible. I did my best to believe that; however, there was something amiss in his story. Still, what did it matter? I had a van and when he was away that meant I could go on adVANtures whenever I pleased. I think what particularly appealed to me about having a van was opportunist naps or 'napportunities' as I called them. With a rock and roll bed, one can nap anywhere especially when the tinted windows concealed there was a nifty napper inside. Although some of my friends made nifty napping less exciting when they called it mobile nana napping.

During the plague, as I called it, I was able to work from home and as wonderful as that was, it meant I was completely isolated and there was no escape from work. It was sitting there, staring at me twenty-four hours a day. My van acquisition came about at the perfect time. I had an alternative space to escape to and I could 'practice' my camping on my parking space outside my flats. Imagine! My neighbours thought I had lost the plot. I explained that all of the hotels were shut. Rather than being able to take a weekend away in a nice hotel there was no break from the same four walls. I was living at work and there was no dodging the fact that one was constantly available. So what else could a person do for a change of scenery - other than go on a camping trip on your own parking space?

What I find funny is how I used to love camping when I was young, but that was when I could do without sleep. Now, in my mid-forties I have the privilege of having to remember the details of hundreds of digital systems, codes, and how these things integrate. On top of that I have to figure out how system architectures talk, and build the equivalent to automated robots into systems. I can't afford to have no sleep because each working day involves running full speed on a mental treadmill. That is commonly labelled success. What it should be labelled is an illusion based on living at full mental capacity on a daily basis to provide a corporation with more effective systems so that they can lay people off. I might be a bit jaded; however, that is what I am privy to. That is the end of the geek talk.

Back to the life-changing tent moment. That weekend camping with some friends really was a game changer. Denise showed us around her van. It had a wooden interior and plenty of bunting. She had purchased Vangelina a few years previously. She was now ten years old. There was something so cosy about the van and there were great views from the windows. Denise could lie in her bed, open the back doors and enjoy the view wherever she had parked up. There was something so very 'life-style' about it.

Denise was in her fifties, had worked and retired. Her husband had died at sixty-two and left her money. She said they had always wanted to buy a van and travel when he retired. So when he passed on she felt she should honour that dream. She invested in the van, and worked part-time making floral arrangements for weddings and funerals. She spent long weekends adVANturing. She said she liked to work and preferred short stints in her van because she liked to be at home as well. The van afforded her regular changes of scenery and a nice place to gather with friends after sea swimming. She said she was living her best life.

After a wonderful campfire and evening under the stars, we retired to our tents. I opened the tent flap and gazed out at the stars. Denise's van had solar fairy lights decorating the outside and the interior. It seemed so homely. In contrast I laid on an inflatable bed which was relatively comfortable. I shifted position and felt quite queasy. I laid flat on my back, adjusted again and my brain felt wobbly like I was sea-sick. In the end I laid still in one position. It then grew cold, I was in a sleeping bag, but it wasn't enough. So that night I opened the tent flaps and drifted in and out of a doze until the 'drunken launch'. There was no way I could sleep after that, so I laid with the tent flap open gazing into proper darkness. The stars were beautiful, the random noises from farm animals was relatively amusing. At the same time I could hear my tented friends fidgeting and sighing in frustration. I glanced over at the van, Denise was cosy, comfy and warm. She had heating. That night I reconciled my finances. I had intended to pay off my mortgage early. The thing was I wanted to live now. There is always that inner conflict of generating savings and living in the present. I felt the universe was saying live now because it had shown me signs. Over the previous months I ran into a lady with the type of van I wanted when I was paddle boarding. She had shown me around. Another couple of my friends had them too. What I liked about them was they were long enough to be a van and short enough to park in a normal parking space. What's more, they weren't so expensive. As much as I would like to go in 'guns a van blazing' and buy something new, I needed to see whether I liked having a van.

A woman I knew from yoga made her husband buy a brand new sixty thousand pound van and… she didn't like it. She couldn't sleep because she felt too confined. Admittedly she was used to five star hotels and spas, but she had thought that having a van would be 'fun'. It wasn't fun for her and vans are not for everyone. I had seen both sides of the coin. Someone who loved their van versus someone who didn't get on with it at all. I did wonder whether the lady who was given a sixty thousand pound van would have learned to love it if she had had to work for it and save the money herself. Oh and something I found fascinating was the lady who didn't like her van never named her. There was no van-connection.

So rather than pay off my mortgage in ten years, I used my savings and ordered a van. I had her converted. When she was ready 'Blossom' was delivered to my parking space. The first drive I fell in love. Yes I fell in love with my van, Blossom. She was a silver elegant beauty with a rock and roll bed, a stove, a fridge, a couple of cupboards and a sink. She symbolised weekend adventures and the opportunity to work from van rather than work from home; although, work from van could be home if you thought about it. Who defines 'home', as long as the work gets done and delivered?

So, back to the crazy thoughts, I had been gali-van-ting over the weekends and finding space just to be. The weekend I lost my vanginity was a turning point. By the way vanginity doesn't mean playing hide the sausage in the van; instead, vanginity is the first time you sleep in the van. So, those same tenting friends and I went to a campsite in the middle of the countryside. By this point all of us had vans or mobile homes. Our lives had shifted to proper van-ity within three months of my bed-launching camping experience. One of the girls had split up with her partner and was already living in her van.

She had toured Scotland and completely re-evaluated her life. She was an adventurous inspiration. Those crazy thoughts may have been influenced by that evening when she talked about sleeping out in remote areas and discovering her ancestry. It was amazing what a fire pit, a decent chilli and fabulously free friends can do for a soul.

After sleeping for five hours in Blossom, which was a record, I had another group of friends to meet out in the forest. We were all taking the opportunity when it presented itself. I arrived in my van and two of the other women, who were being made redundant from one of the big flight companies, said they were thinking about completely changing their lives. I didn't think anything of it because we went on one of those long walks which provided a view of a stag humping, a whole host of birds of prey, horses creating a line across a road and a five mile walk turning into a half marathon due to our navigator feeling that it might be better to take a short cut that added eight miles to the route. We were clearly not lost because you are never lost when you are experiencing new places from a new perspective. So... the crazy thoughts sat dormant but experiencing new places from a new perspective without a time limit became rather appealing.

The two ladies, who were being made redundant, had time, for the first time in their lives. They had worked for the airline for thirty years. Their bodies never recovered from the flight zones and now they were fresh and energised. They could be present and not tired... There was something in that. The rest, the recuperation and the recovery appealed. The time to be able to have headspace to take one's time and enjoy. Plus the desire to not trying to fit everything in rose within me. Imagine going at a gentle pace and enjoying it all – a possibility I had not previously envisioned.

'Sometimes you just have to say stuff it!' one of my friends said. 'I have worked solidly for thirty years. I will possibly retire in twenty, that is, if they don't change the pensionable age again. I intend to take this time out and enjoy it… or find a new way of doing things. I love your van - I think there is something in that. There is freedom and travel opportunity.' That was when a seed was planted. I remember in the book *Man's Search for Meaning* that Victor Frankl had always looked for opportunity. In all honesty, I was happy to have a good job that paid well. I liked the attitude of the company – they intended to get ahead of the competition while everyone else was consumed in fear. That meant pressure increased and the automation delivery and build ramped up too. My intention was to ride the storm until things settled as I had lost everything in 2008 because of the Lehman Brother's collapse. I had lost my photography business and had lost my income. When I finally managed to get a job, the company I worked for went into administration. I had lived on my savings for a year and thank God I had saved. That was a horrid lesson and one that had stayed with me. I had decided that when I got a good job again the least I would save each month was one quarter of my wage – if I could live on a half of my wage then that was going to be the way I accumulated.

It was during my time out of work I read everything I could about money accumulation, money automation and the psychology of wealth. Strangely that knowledge became the foundation for the loan and finance systems I build now. That time taught me all about generating funds, creating passive incomes that accumulate while you are asleep and how the 'Richest Man in Babylon' studied business rather than a craft. Yet, what it doesn't teach you is that it is all very well acquiring wealth, yet your health is the true wealth. As conditioned as we are to chase goals and be successful, there is a deep sense of dissatisfaction. In my opinion, that is down to the fact that we are all so busy and over-stimulated that we have lost a sense of being and a sense of true community. So that question – What if there was a better way to live was the first 'Stuff it!' step. I needed the space and time to figure out 'what is the better way?' When one is in a system, they are unable to see the system. So I realised that I was going to have to step away to figure out a solution. It wasn't going to be an erratic 'Stuff it!' Or a giant 'Look at me - I am saying 'Stuff it!" Instead, it was going to be a calculated, methodical and gradual 'Stuff it!' I intended to complete all my projects, to clean and clear within myself and to prepare for the new. When I made my 'Stuff it!' decision energy rose within me and expanded. I knew it was the right thing, yet, I was consumed in a masculine, logical, technological world. My feminine energy was concealed and trampled by my intellectual capacity and survival in a very logical/analytical environment.

There was a lot to process before the leap and my intention was to write it, document it and record it. I liked the idea of being seventy and watching the me, I once was, go through a process of saying 'Stuff it!' and finding a new way – my way. What made 'Stuffing it!' all the more exciting was that I didn't intend to tell anyone. I just wanted to document and do it my way. I had no need to seek approval, I had no need to ask permission. I just intended to quietly do what I needed to do. I have worked in enough environments where people tell you what they are going to do, they detail everything and talk and talk and talk. Nothing comes of it. Instead, there is something so wonderful about making a decision – a 'Stuff it!' decision and go about making it reality without other people telling you that you are nuts, their opinions, or all the reasons why you shouldn't step into the unknown. I have experienced that before and you realise that people's opinions are nothing personal. Unfortunately many people project their own fears onto you.

As part of the preparation for the 'Stuff it!' next phase, I meditated, I did yoga and worked with concentrated focus. So, I experimented with some of my 'manifestational meditations', to see whether they revealed themselves. Admittedly Blossom was on my vision board and I had wanted a van for over twenty-five years. It was just that I was never in the position to have one, park one or use one. So let's see whether the little voice of 'Stuff it' provided other insights along the way...

CHAPTER 4

THE DECISION

That weekend was my last weekend with Ryan. We rolled out the rock and roll bed for a forest nap. It wasn't romantic at all. Instead he took up most of the bed and I felt squashed. He criticised Blossom and said he would have chosen a larger van with this and that... Of course he would, but he couldn't actually afford a van or a car because apparently his wife had rinsed him during their divorce. The divorce which apparently hadn't taken place, according to his wife. Alarm bells continued ringing because he was always asking to borrow money. I always said no, but it didn't stop him trying. He was that skint that we always had to go halves on food. That should have been enough of an aggravation. How could a forty-eight year old man be in such a sorry financial state? He was also quite odd in his behaviour. None of his stories added up. I asked whether he had seen his ex-wife over the weekend. He said he hadn't seen her at all. Hmmm! He must have kept his eyes closed while he shagged her. Anyway I asked him to book a table at a restaurant in the forest. I intended to take us there because he loved cream teas. When he made the booking he made quite a school-boy error. He booked it under his 'real name'. When we arrived at the restaurant he said that name and I took a mental note. I went to the loo and added his real name to my phone. My gut was churning. He hadn't realised his mistake, but again, I knew it was the beginning of the end. I returned to a cream tea and stories of exes... I listened and paid attention to the patterns while I arranged my jam and cream on the scone. The expression 'Stuff it!' popped into my head 'Stuff him too!' It was a whisper but it made me smile. He noticed my expression as I grinned at the scone.

'I am a jam on the bottom and cream on top kind of girl. You cream your bottom first...' I said, finding myself incredibly amusing.

He glanced at my scone…The expression 'Stuff it!' played through my mind again. Little did I know that whisper would evolve into a scream.

That was the last time I saw him. When I returned home I checked my phone because I had unblocked the 'ex-wife' to see what else she had to say. *'You are desperate aren't you? Well I suggest you stop seeing him. I know where you live...'* she wrote, in a tone of threat.

Some people are really stupid. I guess not everyone realises pretty much everything can be tracked and some people work in data investigation. Admittedly I didn't like to abuse my access; however, being threatened justified what I was about to do. Since I had his real name it was time to unravel the truth about him, his wife, and what they were up to. My gut felt deception and fraud. A little investigation was necessary because the pair were arseholes. It didn't take much to discover they were still married, he had a history of domestic violence and had been done for fraud. From what I could gather the pair worked together. He accessed dating sites and dated numerous women. He would borrow money from dates, shown in his financial transactions. He even had a specific account dedicated to dating financial acquisition. It was in the thousands, not hundreds of thousands; however, it was substantial. The hard luck story and 'let's split the bill' were all part of the 'act'. When he had reached a certain financial acquisition or the date said no to lending money, then the wife would turn up. The date would then dump him. How often do you ask for the money you loaned someone when you dump them? You dump them and accept the loss of any monies related to it. It was a scam to say the least and a relatively clever one because there were always more fish to scam in the dating pond. Ironically there had been a recent surge of such scams and many of the chaps involved had cited they were in the navy. That way they could say they were at sea and had reason to not be available. By doing that they could 'serve' numerous women and acquire more finances. What I couldn't get my head around was how they managed to maintain the lies to so many vulnerable people. I have never been able to understand deception, lies and liars, so always wanted to turf them up so they got their comeuppance.

Anyway, enough of the 'sob story'. So I responded to the wife, told her not to threaten me, dumped Ryan and built a case against them. It was added to an 'investigation'. I didn't need to be named as the originator, there were plenty of potential witnesses should the case go to court. The pair had acquired money from plenty of innocent women who had hoped to find love. They could be contacted should the investigation continue. What's more, the redemption could appear as though it came from out of the blue. Neither of them knew what I did for a living, he knew I worked with code, computers and systems but had no understanding of investigative analytics. Not many people do. Anyway the pair would be put under surveillance and all communications tracked and recorded. Needless to say I changed my locks and my location. I can work from anywhere, although, I like to have a base. In my attempt to trust, I had let him into my home. I didn't feel safe now. He could turn up at any point or so could she. Admittedly they could be tracked but what was the point? In all honesty when something ends there is no point hanging on. Move on! So, I rented a lodge in a remote location and continued working. The thing is working away cuts you off from your friends and that was something I needed after feeling such disappointment. I wondered why, as an honest person, I would attract such a wombat into my life. When such things happen, I throw myself into work, and work more hours. I had separated myself from my normal life which made the whole sense of 'Stuff it!' resonate through my being. Maybe I just needed a break to completely re-evaluate and re-set. I wanted to be away from screens, be reminded of the beauty in life, wonderful people, and wanted to spend time in nature. 'Stuff it!' had gone from a whisper into a continuous haunting. I tried to block it out. However, when you wake up in the morning and your brain starts singing 'Stuff it, stuff it, stuff it…' you wonder whether you are going nuts. The next thing you know, you are humming the 'Stuff it!' song! What made it worse was the song was getting louder. At one point I had a dream where there was a 'Stuff it!' yodel competition across a valley. It is quite a challenge to yodel the word 'Stuff it!' I woke up laughing a couple of times because of it. Imagine dreaming of opening your front door to a group of carol singers singing 'We wish you a merry 'Stuff it!' and a Happy adVANturous new year...' My unconscious wasn't going to let it go.

Everywhere I went I would be reminded to 'Stuff it!' In the end I accepted I had to make the decision, although in truth that decision had already been made. 'Stuff it!' was going to haunt me until I fully actioned the 'Stuff it!' and did what needed to be done. I had to let work know that I intended to 'Stuff it!' and go on a proper adVANture. It wasn't about finding myself, instead, it was about enjoying, going slowly and being in awe once more. The adVANture was about emptying the mind of the endless busy and recalibrating, to move forwards. The only challenge was allowing myself time. 'STUFF IT!'

CHAPTER 5

STUFFING IT GOOD AND PROPER

I finally decided to say 'STUFF IT!' (like I had to decide) and there was a timeframe involved. As with all goals we have to make a decision and have a deadline. As much as I would like to waft along and let things unfold, that never happens or works for me. Instead, I have to have clarity and know what I am aiming for. If I was going to run a marathon I would train for a marathon over a period of time and then on the day of the marathon I would be ready. Of course some would do a bit of running here and there and randomly run a marathon. That would piss me off. I like my structure, I like my order, and I like my discipline. That is how I deliver and make my company happy. My creative endeavours are hobbies that turn up in the form of books, children's books and creative writing… So I decided on a six month 'stuffing it' timeframe. Before the intended departure date there would be some practice 'Stuff its!' where I would spend time in the van and see what needs to be refined.

The approach was similar to building a system, a piece of technology or an app, and put it into a test environment to see whether it works and where all the bugs are. When you know where the bugs are you then fix them before releasing the system, app or technology into the world. In my case I intended to see how it felt to live van life and adventure for a few short stints and build up my number of van-tastic nights. I might hate it. I might recoil and reverse the 'Stuff it!' Although, on the other hand, I may well love 'Stuffing it', figure out that I need certain equipment or van-cessories before a truly epic 'Stuff it' commences.

I realised I like the idea of an off-grid 'Stuff it!' Ohhhhh now that made me feel excited. An epic 'Stuff it!' Yey!!! To step away and live a life of adventure and be free of corporations and hierarchy. That is what happens when you say 'I am outta here' in your head. Your brain starts to imagine all the brochure images such as frolicking around in remote places and talking to butterflies.

The thing with 'stuffing it' is the dream versus the reality. The mini 'Stuff its!' work up to the ultimate 'Stuff it!' and will provide an insight into hidden costs. I also worked on figuring out how one can have either enough money to extend the Stuff it, or receive income while perpetually 'Stuffing it!' I could see how this journey wanted to unfold. What's more, I liked the idea of the 'Stuff it fund' or 'Stuff it savings'. This isn't a rainy day fund. Instead this is the fund that allows you to walk away from any bullshit. The 'Stuff it fund' gives you the power to say 'No!' When you are reliant on a job then the company realises they can shaft you. Imagine having a fund that enables to stop taking any crap and tell your bosses to shove it up their arses or stuff it up their arses... One of my friends calls it the 'F*off fund'. Whichever way you wish to say the same thing... However saying 'Stuff it up your arses is highly satisfying'. Anyway your 'Stuff it!' delivery is entirely up to you and I know saying 'Stuff it up your arses' is completely crass, completely unprofessional; however, there are polite ways to tell a company and/or bosses that their rectum is the suitable place for them to stuff it. I might be delighting in an imaginary journey!

I am sure that many of you lovelies, like me, have learned to corporately smile while the image of telling the company to shove it has stampeded through your mind. It usually happens at bonus time or pay reviews when the company have demonstrated a complete lack of appreciation and taken advantage. The thing is I really like my job and figuring out how to build technology to detect liars, fraudsters and scammers. Ultimately I am going to STUFF IT! But I think it might be a nice stuff it. I have burned my bridges before... In fact when I say burn, it could have been likened to an inferno. I won't do that again. In the meantime, it is time to make a plan. Where do I want to visit? What would I like to see? What do I desire to experience? Sometimes the planning is more fun than the adventure because there is all of the imagining involved. Imagination - the magical vision of possibility! Yipeeeeee!

CHAPTER 6

PLAN/PLANS AND PLANNING

A person without a plan is really a person without a plan; however, they always say without a plan one plans to fail. I think that some people are planners and some people go with the flow. No matter what the approach you take you will end up somewhere. One will arrive based on thinking their plan took them to the goal, the other will arrive in a state of bewilderment or maybe they are always simply where they are at a given moment in time. Does it matter? The truth is you only arrive at a point if life allows you to. The illusion is thinking that we are actually in control. I have worked in many jobs and careers… The career plan is laid and out and… boom shaka-laka the company folds, an unprecedented set of events take place or personal circumstances change, such as winning the lottery. No one has any idea what is in store for them; yet there is a sense of reassurance in creating a plan or having an idea about what you would like to experience.

Although, back to the world of corporate; my favourite question in an interview: 'Where do you see yourself in five years?' I have to contain my laughter, clearly they haven't read my C.V/Resume. One minute I am a Vice President of a High profile financial company, the next I am an expedition leader in Antarctica. Currently I am a Business Analyst building mini-robots into financial systems using some of the best coders/developers around to figure out who are scammers, fraudsters and hackers. 'Where do you see yourself in five years?'

Stupid bloody question – if someone can see themselves doing something in five years then they really need security or fear change. In this current world, and financial climate, where chaos rules and survival is about adaptability, bigger vision and taking leaps, then the person who can see themselves staring at a screen doing exactly the same thing is deluded... unless they have set it up to do that precise thing on a specific date in five years.

So now that I have dismissed planning I am going to put an evolving plan together.

PLAN A – Stuff it

PLAN B – Shit myself and stay safe.

PLAN C – Laugh like a film baddy and see what unexpected randomness takes place.

The journey - It is simple and I have now purchased a map of funny place names. I live in Bournemouth and there are some lovely place names on the way to Cornwall such as Happy Bottom, Slap Bottom and Shitterton. That in itself is a journey that will put a smile on my face. It is like the journey is a bit of an intestinal meandering. There are some really lovely places around Dorset, so I think I am going to do some small drives between nice places. I have realised that I have to let work know and that means the fantasy is about to become reality. That is where the anxiety begins. All of the worst case scenarios play through your mind. You hand your notice in and can't find another job, ever. You then have to sell your van and live for the rest of your life eating rats. I don't know whether I mentioned that having an analytical and creative brain is both a curse and a joy. One can imagine great beauty and be tormented by some rather convoluted worst-case scenarios. The problem with such mentality is that you can over-think and think yourself right out of doing something. What's more, when you are making a plan you can over research, look at all of the imagery and then think what is the point? I know that is weird but I am not the only one who does that.

I am aware I just deviated again from where I want to go. So, I want to go to Scotland, and Cornwall to Scotland is quite a biggy, so there will have to be stops on the way. I intend to take my paddle board, so the Lake District makes sense and I like the look of Glastonbury too. A nice stop in the Cotswolds would break up the journey. I have always wanted to go to Northumberland, so it looks like up the left side of the country as far as the isle of Skye, across Scotland to Glencoe/Glenmore and then down past Edinburgh to Northumberland and down towards Buxton, Bath and then home. I reckon that is about three months if done at a nice gradual pace. Three months to cover my mortgage, my travels and expenditure equates to around seven thousand pounds with no income. Hmmm. It is when one starts to consider costs that the fear builds. What if I don't get a job on my return? What if I have to eat rats? Should I rent out my place? Ahhhh the mental overwhelm!

When my brain goes into an eruption of asteroids I have to walk... the rhythm brings me back to being. So, I walked. If I saved half of my wages for the next three months and used savings I could do the trip, not rent out my place and have three months to find another job. That night was my last night to finalise everything in my mind and to hand in my notice the following day. I had to give three months' notice; so that night was my last night of mental churn before making the leap… Frightened? That was an understatement.

CHAPTER 7

WE CAN DO THIS THE EASY WAY OR THE HARD WAY

The sense of dread in my stomach that morning was horrible. I took a deep breath before phoning H.R. The chap in charge was a decent chap and an adventurer too. So I took a deep breath and dialled through a digital platform and had a video call. He quickly picked up and the banter began. He said he sensed something brewing. So I was honest and said that in three months I intended to go on an adVANture. He was very excited for me, but less excited for work. He asked how long I intended to go for. I said two to three months. He seemed to be calculating. He asked whether there was a particular reason that I wanted to leave the company. I said there wasn't I just didn't have enough holiday to cover such a trip. He said that he just needed to make some calls and could he call back in an hour. I found that rather strange. Still, he was a decent chap and I agreed. As I said I like my job, the company I work for is technological, innovative and has a progressive attitude. That was why I worked for them, I might have been a woman in my mid-forties (a lot older than the young coders and developers in the company) however they respected me and my experience.

An hour later H.R called back. He had talked to the head of the company, who definitely had his own way of doing things. He also saw the big picture and took different angles at problem solving. So, as always, he called my bluff. So John was honest, he said clearly that it would cost more money to employ and train someone in what I do when they couldn't be guaranteed to deliver. He said we could do this the hard way or the easy way. The big boss always focused on easy and simple rather than struggle and complex. As much as he was demanding he knew his stuff and certainly was a genius. So John said, how would you feel about using up part of your holiday and then taking the rest unpaid? That way you could have two months unpaid and one month paid. That would take you until the beginning of August if you leave in May. Half of me wanted to think about it. Yet my mouth answered before my brain. 'Yes,' I said. So my great 'STUFF IT!' was more of a gentle 'Stuff it!' I didn't need to throw everything in the air and make a giant show of it all. Instead, I could subtly 'Stuff it!' and go on a lovely adVANture knowing that I had financial security. Maybe it could be a soft 'Stuff it!' before a slightly larger 'STUFF IT!' until I reached the heady heights of a 'STUUUUUUFFFF ITTTT!'

John seemed pleased that I didn't want to leave the company. He said they would have to write a policy so the other staff also had an opportunity to do such things. He asked for me to keep my potential adventures to myself until they had written the policy because they didn't want an influx of staff requesting to head for the hills on a whim.

That afternoon I advised my director of my plan and she wasn't surprised. She had worked with me in my previous company where I worked six month contracts. When I came to the end of a contract I would go off on a random trip such as across Japan on bullet trains, a tour around Mauritius, or a rather nice tree house trip across Thailand where everywhere I stayed had to be in a tree house… I know… I like to be a bit random and set a theme. She was always a bit bemused by the fact I just went on such trips and then returned for the next contract. Unfortunately my days of big abroad adventures had been scuppered by the international plague. I didn't want to sit on a plane or be in confined spaces with other people. That is another reason I was happy when I bought Blossom. I could be in an open space and nicely contained. Also during the lockdowns Blossom provided an alternative space to just 'be' and worked as a change of scenery. I have to admit, I grew to love Blossom and the fact she felt so nurturing. Every time I sat in her I felt at home – safe, and there was potential. She certainly became my pride and joy. I hung star fairy lights inside and could potter about in her for hours.

Anyway, I'm deviating. That afternoon I received an email from H.R stating that they were aware that I intended to take some paid and unpaid leave for a three month duration. It would commence on the 1st May and end on the 1st August, where I would return to full-time work. There was a document attached, which I was to sign and it was done. There was no bureaucracy and no big resignations, instead my 'Stuff it!' gracefully flowed, all I had to do now was plan the trip, book the trip and go. I had three months. I had enough savings to do it well because I had a job to return to.

While we are on the subject of money: I will provide a little insight into the way I handle finances, and this came from a huge lesson in 2008, where I nearly lost everything. So basically one needs to have a rainy day fund. That is a minimum of three months' wages to live on. There also needs to be a small 'fun fund' – which I call the Spa jar. This has twenty pounds a week automatically paid into it. I have a bills account where I have an automatic feeder that puts ten percent more than is necessary a month into an account to cover all bills and eventualities. I then have savings and a 'Stuff it' account. Yep... I know it sounds very controlled but when you have reached a state where you are on your last five pounds and thinking 'Shit... What am I going to do?' You learn a very hard lesson, and that was when I started trying to live on half of my monthly wage and dispersing the rest into the above accounts. The 'Stuff it fund' was born into reality when I worked for a company that paid great money but was run by some absolute ****s. You can fill in your own word there. The thing is I was trapped in a golden handcuff situation where I had plenty of money but ridiculous stress levels. That was when I decided that I would save, pay off the mortgage and be able to say 'Stuff it' whenever I felt like it. I had worked building debt systems and I saw what debt did to people. That motivated me to make the decision to be debt-free, mortgage-free, and not beholden to anyone. What is strange, is that as I write this, it seems that the essence of 'Stuff it!' has been lurking in my unconscious for years and in many forms. In this instance, my current 'Stuff it!' has unfolded in the most unexpected way and in the easiest way. I definitely felt blessed and valued.

CHAPTER 8

THE GNOME SANCTUARY

'I may have said something a bit odd to the head of the company regarding your trip...' My Director, Teresa sounded awkward and apologetic. 'You know how you sent me pictures of that map with *Devil's Arse, Twat and Muff as places to visit?'*

I could feel the blood drain from my face. 'Well we were in a meeting with the other executives and they asked why you needed to go away for three months. That map flashed into my head. I could hardly say you were visiting *Muff, Twat and Devil's Arse* could I?'

'Oh no... What did you say?' I asked in a tone filled with cringe.

'Well I was in a bit of a panic... All I could see was the word TWAT in big letters so... I said you were visiting a Gnome Sanctuary,' she said, as though it was the most natural alternative.

Silence was the only response. Teresa had told the executives and owner of the company that I needed to take three months off to visit a Gnome Sanctuary! Well what could be a more obvious reason to take three months off?

'So what did they say?' I asked.

'Well there was a long drawn out silence and Michael (the head of the company) said *'Well she is a bit odd isn't she?'* Teresa sounded rather amused.

What do you say to that? There had been other occasions where I was dealing with the owner of the company and had a weird series of events unfold. One particular one jumped out at me when Teresa, Michael and I had been on a call regarding a system mapping where I was showing him the fraud vulnerabilities. In the banter Terrassa mentioned I had a campervan. Bear in mind the man is a billionaire. He seemed intrigued and asked 'What's the best thing about having a campervan?'

Teresa cut in, 'She cooks sausages… There's nothing that Ruby likes better than a good sausage in her campervan.' There was nothing malicious in what she said, she just hadn't realised the 'hide the sausage' connotations. I actually wonder why Michael had made such allowances to enable me to stay with the company. He was probably in a state of sausage suspense, wondering what weird shit Teresa was going to come up with about me next. Anyway, life provided opportunity and all I had to do now was plan and prepare… The countdown was on and the itinerary drafted.

New Forest-> Bere Regis -> Eype -> Golden Cap -> Dartmoor -> Gwithian -> Glastonbury -> Poole (My friend's birthday) -> Cotswolds -> Lake District -> Galloway -> Clattering's Shaw -> Highlands Way -> Loch Lomond -> The Journey across Glencoe -> Glenmore/Avimore -> Northumberland -> Buxton -> Bath -> New Forest.

CHAPTER 9

LOSING YOUR VANGINITY

When I mention vanginity many people think I am talking about having a shag in the van. Nope that is not it at all. There is something bigger and far more meaningful than that. Instead you lose your vanginity the night that you first sleep out in the van. You see when you buy a van you have all of these lovely Instagram images of luxury sleeping, comfort and warmth and… the reality is that you generally freeze, end up in a storm or realise that you need to have a proper memory foam cover for your bed, especially if it is a rock and roll bed. Then there are the simple things like hooking up the gas and how the heating works. So with all of that in mind, my vanginity was lost on a hillside near Wareham in Dorset. My friend had found a great campsite where we could have a fire pit and gaze out at the stars. It was close enough for some lovely walks and a short drive to the Tank Museum. Who doesn't want to go and visit a Tank Museum?

So this site was made up of open fields, had some electrical hook-ups and some very good showers. My first big trip was in March and you might be forgiven for thinking that it wouldn't be that cold. Oh and that was the learning. Even when you are in a van you can get cold. That one trip provided a massive learning. My fear was that I would not sleep. Sleep is so precious to me because in my work I have to be alert, detailed and able to function. The potential of a long sleepless weekend was terrifying. Anyway, I arrived on Friday night to be greeted by three of my vanning friends and their vans. These are part of the same group that camped that night in tents. Within three months all of us had purchased our vans. Angelina purchased Van Morrison, it was was a late 1990's van, which reminded me of an old style bed and breakfast. It was super comfy and when the bed was set up three people could comfortably sleep there. The thing was setting up the bed was a bit of a hassle and my friend often slept on one side making it a single. Van Morrison had a toilet, a warm shower and a kitchen with a cooker. There was bunting, mandalas and crystals arranged nicely inside. It suited my friend who had exchanged corporate life to become a healer. She intended to spend time at festivals doing readings, healings and sleeping in her van. It was perfect for her.

Higgedy's name came from his number plate. Sheena bought Higgedy for five thousand pounds. He was twenty years' old and well used. She had re-upholstered him, but I feared for the engine. He worked well enough; although, it didn't have longevity. Sheena, didn't have any spare disposable income and had literally sold every available item she had on Ebay to raise the funds for interior decoration. She had arrived at a point where she had nothing left to sell. She was a single mum of three boys, so she had her work cut out. The fact she had managed to find something in that budget range that didn't need completely gutting was phenomenal. When you stepped inside she had created the most beautiful interior and it felt like home. She was excellent at handicraft and beading, so had made an interior like no other. It was like stepping into a French boudoir filled with beautiful beads. I half expected Moulin Rouge dancers to emerge from the bathroom and can can out into the field.

We then had Jana, she still had her super comfy van and felt like she was a proud mother of a group of young vaneers all stepping into van life together. 'A van will change you in profound ways,' she said. She was right. 'Each van has its own personality and reveals a lot about its owner and their inner world.'

Her van was plush, pillows plumped and everything was in good order. Everything had a place and that place was perfect. Her storage solutions were classy and clever.

Finally there was Blossom, a Japanese import that I had had converted. She had a fridge, a cooker, a sink and a hidden porta potty. Space was efficient and limited. I had a rock and roll bed, a Captain's swivel chair and enough space for me. Efficiency, details and design were the fundamentals of Blossom. She was an elegant, well designed beauty with an efficient and clever interior concealed by tinted windows. Her awning was the only revealing feature that might make a passer-by consider she was a campervan because her original purpose was as an executive people carrier from Japan. She was adaptable, powerful and secretive. She was everything I needed in a van.

That night was my vanginity rite of passage. We sat together around the fire pit, ate vegan chilli con carnie (not advised for losing your vanginity) and laughed about the randomness of our lives. I had recently returned to being single. Sheena was getting divorced. Jana had multiple lovers and Angelina had dating carnage. That night was a full moon, there was a rainbow around the moon because it was freezing. The sky was clear and the stars were twinkling. It was wonderful. I will be honest, I am a woose when it comes to late nights. I wake up at five-thirty, so I was the first to go to bed and that was when I discovered my first school-girl error. That night there was a light breeze and I had parked under an oak tree. I felt all smug and went to switch on my van heating and... 'error'. It seemed I did not have enough power to maintain the fridge and have the heating on at the same time. I was a bit confused because I had electrical hook-up. I later learned I hadn't switched on the EHC. I had hooked up but not 'pressed on'.

Can you imagine you have just set up your bed and you have to put on a thermal hat? You can see your breath inside the van and you have a sleeping bag and blanket but the reality is that's not going to be enough. At midnight it was zero degrees by dawn it was at least minus two possibly minus four.

There is nothing fun about freezing. So the first thing I realised is that I had to move the van from under the oak tree. Now, there is a bit of an unspoken rule on campsites. You don't switch your engine on after a certain time. Usually it is around 10.30pm. The thing is even though I had electrical hook-up I hadn't bought a heater. So there was a combination of two things. I needed to heat the van and I needed to move it. So I switched on the engine and drove forwards but kept the engine on to heat the van.

What is amazing about Blossom is she is very quiet, and you can separately heat the front and rear of the van. There are controls for both. So I whacked up the heating. My friend came and knocked on the window and asked if everything was okay. I told her I was frozen and that the acorns were landing on my roof. She pulled a face and said, 'Just be aware you are likely to piss a few people off by turning on your engine. I got it and I learned that lesson. Admittedly someone switching on their engine while I was trying to sleep would have pissed me off too. That isn't justifying it... Well it is a bit... I just wanted to put it in perspective, it wasn't like revving a Harley Davidson or firing up a Ferrari. Instead, it would have been a subtle murmur. Anyway, I reached a stable heat, climbed into my sleeping bag and laid on two roll-out mattresses. They weren't terribly comfortable but were better than sleeping on the seat of the pure roll-out bed. I realised at that point it was worth investing in a proper memory foam cover. I re-arranged and placed my large down jacket over the top of the mattresses which created a buffer. I laid back down and fell asleep instantly.

During the night my friends continued laughing and giggling until around three in the morning. They were night owls and I was an early bird. We had accepted that none of us would change a long time ago. They were definitely louder than my engine, so I sensed we were going to get 'looks' the following day.

Well I woke up at 6.30, which was a lie in for me. The sun was rising, it was freezing. I wiped the condensation off my back window and gazed out... A mist hung over the fields and the golden hues of early morning decorated the surrounding oaks. I laid in my sleeping bag unable to feel my feet or the end of my nose. I felt stiff. The kid's mattresses I had laid over the top of my rock and roll bed weren't enough to make it really comfortable. I wish I had known that before. On top of that it was minus two outside. My sleeping bag accommodated five degrees. I glanced around and my windows were covered in condensation. In some areas it had frozen. I kept my sleeping bag covering me, sat up and put the kettle on. Coffee and dark chocolate would definitely solve the problem. The view was beautiful and I was desperate for the loo. In my haste I had forgotten to set up the porta potty in the night. That was another tip and sequence I had to remember. That meant I was going to have to retract the bed to the get the porta loo out. What's more, the mini mattresses covering the bed, the jacket and the sleeping bag were going to have to be removed. That way I could fold the bed to get into the cupboard where the porta potty was stored. That was another learning... Always get the porta loo out before preparing the bed – get your sequences and orders together!

Okay, so I was being lazy and cold, so, and I don't like to admit this, I got a large paper cup and... yep I peed in it. No one would know. Or so I thought. Anyway the bloody thing steamed. It looked like hot tea, albeit a very yellow one. Thank goodness I had dark windows.

Although I hadn't covered the windscreen. That was another thing that I needed to invest in before any big trips – a screen cover. In the summer the sun rose around four and I can tell you the slightest bit of light bothers me. So, I had to get a decent memory foam mattress topper and screen covers. One only learns by doing and so far in doing I had learned loads.

CHAPTER 10

TEST, TEST AND ONE MORE TEST

Prior to making the big trip I felt that I had a few things to iron out and that meant that I needed to do another test run to sort out any glitches. Thank goodness I did too. Losing my vanginity hadn't been that smooth. There wasn't anything romantic about it... and when my friend knocked my paper cup filled with pee off the 'work surface' there was a somewhat awkward moment. 'That wasn't green tea was it?' she asked with concern on her face. I shook my head. 'Your first piss-mistake,' she grinned. 'Oh don't worry,' I have had worse.

One night had revealed my sleeping bag was not warm enough, the heating I had invested in was temperamental and loud, and my mattress cover wasn't as comfortable as I had hoped. I needed some form of heating, especially when the temperature dropped below zero degrees. Switching on the engine in the middle of the night to get some heat into the van was a major camping faux pas. As much as I could justify my reasoning – it is definitely a first timer's fail. So with that in mind, I felt I had to make another test. Pre-test I invested in some wonderful roll-out memory foam single mattresses. I purchased two, which moulded together. When I placed them over the rock and roll bed and laid on them, I realised they were as comfortable as my bed at home. I was really glad I bought them – I needed to make the experience as comfortable as possible. In addition, I had purchased a sleeping bag which could keep you alive at minus twenty degrees. I learned that hot water bottles were a life-saver because they saved you having to use body heat to get the sleeping bag warm. My brother used to jump around for a while until he was hot before getting into a sleeping bag. If I did that I would be awake because I had blood pumping around my body… So I went for two hot water bottles because my back generally gets cold. Another thing I invested in were thermal blackout screens. It was amazing how quickly warmth drained out of glass. Finally, I purchased a front screen wrap to blackout both the front screen and side windows, because previously head lamps in the night had disturbed my sleep.

So, with all of that learned, I went off into the camping wilderness – well it wasn't actual wilderness – instead it was a forest site with electrical hook-up – I had a back-up fan heater 'just in case'. That may sound extreme for camping in April but I am that person who is always cold and I really don't like it. I have been known to sit in my office wearing a fur hat and a coat when something went wrong with the heating. What made the situation amusing was when I left the hat on my desk, someone mistook it for a cat and thought I had left my cat to guard my desk… The point was I get cold easily and being cold ruins the experience. With regards to hats, I didn't wear a fur hat in bed; however, I did take my thermal hat 'just in case'.

That night I arrived at my electrical hook-up pitch and was delighted with it because it was beside some lovely oak trees and away from people. Now I should have known then that something was afoot because this particular campsite was relatively quiet for the weekend at the beginning of April. So that evening I heated the van using the fan heater, luxuriated with a lovely dinner cooked on my stove, put the star fairy lights on and gazed out at the forest. I actually relaxed and enjoyed some proper quiet. Prior to going to bed, I went for a stroll around in my hooded blanket and felt incredibly cosy. I gazed at the moon, which shone brightly and was astounded by the clusters of stars because they were so clear due to the lack of street lights. The moon had a frosted rainbow around it and I still missed a very important point – it was going to get really cold! In terms of test, that night was extreme because the temperature fell to minus four. Was I cold? Actually I was surprised. My nose was a bit nippy but the sleeping bag and hot water bottle combination did wonders and I slept from ten until eight in the morning, which is unheard of for me. I usually wake up at five-thirty to the roar of traffic noise. Strangely, I didn't need the loo in the night because that would have resulted in a frigid bottom. Not one of my favourite things! Admittedly when I did use the loo in the morning steam rose and I could see my breath. In general I leave a small gap in the front windows to enable fresh air and I did do that; however, there was still condensation but not the usual condensation because it was a sheet of ice.

When I opened the door to take in the view – the cold hit me like a plank. It was a shock – it was bitter outside and there was a heavy frost. Grass crunched beneath one's feet as I walked in the direction of the toilet block. I will be honest, I wanted toilet options when doing my first lone test since losing my vanginity. After the paper cup catastrophe, I thought the test might be easier with a toilet block within walking distance. Admittedly I did use my porta potty, but that was in the evening.

As I walked across the site I took in the view of trees with ice, frozen mist and a golden glowing sun. The atmosphere was magical. I actually felt recharged and refreshed – although one could not help feeling refreshed because the cold was so intense. I wore my hooded blanket, which isn't at all sexy but so comfortable and cosy. I will be honest, for the first time in a long time I relaxed. I had been anxious about sleep deprivation because I intended to do three nights in a row. In that moment my inner world felt content – I knew I could do it. I would return to Blossom, use my 12V portable coffee machine and indulge in dark chocolate for breakfast, well it was a pre-breakfast but that was not the point. My whole intention for the test experience was for total pleasure and so far it was. Everything I had invested in had come up trumps and I cannot state what a difference the memory foam mattresses made. The fact the two mattresses rolled and could be stowed made them a real asset, plus I did not ache. All in all that long weekend was wonderful. TEST=SUCCESS! Yipeeee!

CHAPTER 11

A PRE-TRIP VANCIDENT

In preparation for the big trip I set up my out of office and headed out to the van to potter around and to make sure everything was in place.

Some evenings I would simply go and sit in my van on my parking space and read my book. It is a lovely change of scenery. Anyway the darkened windows seem to have a gravitational pull because they have drawn quite a few people/neighbours from the flats to press their faces against the window and peer in whether it is daylight or night.

That night it was stormy, pelting with rain and I glanced up from my book. I screamed! It looked like the grim reaper was peering in the window! After catching my breath, I realised it was my elderly neighbour peering in wearing a black poncho and carrying one of those dog-ball throwing sticks which resembled a scythe. It turned out that her pup had pooped outside my van so she was searching for the puppy poop and in doing so had risen up just as the security light back-lit her.

The following day another vancident unfolded. Isn't it bizarre that a person could have been driving for twenty-six years and one month before their big trip they get a speeding ticket? That was the first speeding ticket I ever had. I was going 34 miles an hour along a local road in urgent acquisition of a pastry because I hadn't had breakfast. I will be honest, I was particularly hungry and the hunger seemed to overwhelm my acceleration pedal. I needed the chocolate croissant and coffee. Was it worth the fine and what unfolded? Hmmm.

There is a moment when you sense you have been caught. Something in the back of my mind registered the camera and that I was over the speed limit. At that moment I didn't care... I just wanted that pastry. The thing is one small instance created some repercussions. What I find astounding is the speed that a speeding ticket comes through. When someone wants money from you it seems that everything is done at a pace. When it comes to wanting a rebate or being charged for something incorrectly or even contesting a fine then have you noticed it takes ages? Well, that speeding ticket arrived with some options. In this particular case I could have points added to the license or I could take part in a driver awareness course for over one hundred pounds. I thought I would take the driver awareness course, the thing was I was running out of time and phoned them up because I just had a couple of weeks before departing on the journey I would not have definite Wi-Fi signal. What's more, I did not want the thought of attending the course hanging over my head.

I have to say that I am glad I took the course. It was funny because I felt like a naughty child when I logged on. The course was done remotely and had course materials. Some of which needed to be read prior to the course. It seemed that many of the participants were just a few miles an hour over the limit and had been also been caught on local roads.

Now, one of the questions on the course was 'How do you rate your driving on a scale of one to ten?' I put myself at six because I am an average driver. I am not terribly confident and I spend an enormous amount of time being lost, which means circling roundabouts numerous times. What surprised me was the rest of the course thought they were nine or tens. That got me thinking... If everyone thinks they are really good drivers, we are on roads full of deluded people in control of fast moving vehicles. What made the conversation most interesting was why people thought they were good drivers? Some said it was because they had been driving a long time. Others said they had good cars that they knew how to manoeuvre. Others said they hadn't crashed which made them believe they were very capable. The thing is if people think they are good drivers then they can justify being wombats and making erratic driving decisions. In the end the course was quite brilliant. It talked about where most crashes take place and it seems that most traffic accidents take place locally because drivers switch off because they know the area. It is when they are on auto-pilot that many road incidents take place. That was quite a revelation because I had assumed that most traffic accidents either took place on country lanes or on motorways. Not so.

After a couple of hours of learning and driving refreshers, I came to the conclusion that I really enjoyed the course. I was surprised by how much I had learned. The course strangely provided me with insights about driving and how to drive on difficult and unknown roads. They had a talking aloud technique where you state what you are seeing. That way you maintain focus. I had no idea how that would serve me later on in my trip. There were some terrifying roads ahead and that simple technique kept me focused and enabled me to navigate some gut-wrenching edgy roads in remote areas.

In a strange way that pastry-motivated speeding ticket was a blessing in disguise. What's more, the course was worth the money. It gave me confidence and prepared me for the journey ahead. As I have said I don't pertain to be a good driver. I am an aware driver; however, being in a van and circling roundabouts five or six times to work out the correct route often makes me feel a little driving inept. I am fine with that, although I am sure onlookers might be somewhat bemused to watch my beautiful van pass by numerous times.

CHAPTER 12

THE END OF RUSHING

Three months off means you should be able to take your time. I realise now that I was completely fatigued on a level of soul weariness. All I did was work, work and do more work. It was funny how I became accustomed to that. I fitted life in around work and got up at five in the morning to paddle board, do yoga or go to the beach. All very simple but it rejuvenated the soul. The thing was, I was definitely running on empty and had grown used to living like that. I had been so consumed by all the 'to do lists' that I had not considered the affect that freedom would have on me.

That sense of freedom: isn't it amazing how we can take freedom for granted until it is removed. Now that we can step outside without guilt – how do you truly enjoy that prospect? What is it you love? What is it you desire to experience? What ignites you? What illuminates your soul and puts a smile on your face? I have learned that pleasure is in simplicity… The simplicity of nature. It is taking time out from a hectic work schedule and appreciating life. Slowing down and just being. Being in silence. Being happy. Just being present with the beauty that surrounds us. I love spending time in Blossom, on a paddle board and in nature. I am happy sharing those experiences with friends or family or spending time alone. I love the silence while not thinking about the emails, the deadlines and the demands. I am not concerned by what I should be doing… Who came up with that 'should' for me. It wasn't me…

Well, I could feel myself winding down. Something in me was preparing for the new. Instead I tuned in and enjoyed the moment. I concentrated on the magnificence that surrounded me, that so many miss by being absorbed in the inane. By doing that regularly I elevated my mood and realised it was probably worth sharing. In the meantime I stopped being bothered by work because the two week countdown had begun.

CHAPTER 13

PRACTISING ADVANTURING - A VAN WITH A VIEW

Since I had two weeks left, I had to keep myself occupied and wanted to practice being in Blossom as much as possible. This meant that after work or before work I would take myself off to locations close by and simply indulge in my van-der-lust locally. On one particular occasion, I parked up beside the beach early in the morning and simply had a nice steaming coffee. All the while, watching the world and its weird wonders.

I looked at the temperature on my dashboard. It was ten degrees. The sea was around eleven degrees and a crowd of bathers gathered at seven in the morning. A moment later the group gained momentum and dashed into the sea like a mass of penguins avoiding an elephant seal. Shrill screams and hollers filled the air as frigid water sloshed lady gardens and men's manhoods. It was crevice carnage. Please note the cold water dunking takes place without a wetsuit!

Some thoughts on cold water dunking: I really don't get it? Why would anyone feel the desire on a cold frosty morning to go and dunk themselves in the sea? Where I live it has become 'a thing'. It seems many have been influenced by a chap called Wim Hof and his ice bucket antics. He literally sits in a bucket full of ice. It appears possible that by freezing your nether regions off you feel truly alive. Personally I feel alive without a cold water dunk. The thing is this new thing fascinates me. I quite often take my coffee to the pier and sit watching a group of delirious cold-water dunking ducklings in human form wildly dunk. They stand up to their chests in freezing water doing random breathing techniques. When they are complete they all saunter out of the water with skin the colour of a tomato. It is like they have sunburn.

Of course curiosity generally gets the better of me and I have to ask people why they do it. Soooo here are some answers:

- You really feel present when you do it.
- It is a mental challenge.
- It makes your nervous system function better.
- You reach states of bliss.
- You feel so good.

No one mentioned their iced undercarriage, or the fact they end up screaming the moment the cold hits certain areas, or the fact that hypothermia is likely if you stay in too long. As much as they have justified their whys, does it appeal? Nope. Instead I am going to enjoy the 'now' and not do much... that of course results in thoughts. All those people who dash into the cold water love doing it. It is their passion. Some people view it as madness and others completely don't see where there is any enjoyment. I realised the same was true for adVANturing and van-der-lust. Not everyone gets it. When you look at it from the outside you are essentially kipping in your car in a remote location with strangers. I will be honest, that thought tickled me. AdVANturing isn't for everyone thank goodness and nor is the cold water dunk. As much as I thought I might want to record the build up to the Big AdVANture, I decided I couldn't take the suspense. After packing the van, repacking the van, and then checking I had everything, I started filling up with the 'just in case' items. There is always a state 'I will take it just in case...' 'Just in case' leads to overly crammed cupboards and a whole host of stress. The thing is when your cupboards are jammed full you can't be bothered to go in them to find those 'just in case' items. What's more, the 'just in case' items are usually at the back and at the bottom of a cupboard. So my most ridiculous 'just in case' item – was a rather lovely cake umbrella made of netting and decorated with fake daisies. It really was quite a find and rather beautiful. Admittedly the thought behind the 'just in case cake net,' was good but the reality was that soon after I purchased the beauty I stored it in a cupboard and somehow it got squashed. A few of the arms were bent and it was not quite the visual joy it once was when fresh and new. It made me realise there is a certain amount of discipline required to not over-pack and 'just-in-case' it. In the week leading up to departure, I was meticulous about what I actually needed and 'weeded' the cupboards. The final work day arrived, everything was in order and ready. I felt excited, exhilarated and READY. I had followed the work protocol, had put my out of office on and could feel the tingle of anticipation through my being. I was sooooooo excited. The road ahead was filled with possibility.

CHAPTER 14

HOOPING AND WHOOPING

And so the adVANture began. Yipeeeeee! Now many people would decide to finish work on the Friday, pack up that evening and go the following day. I will be honest, I just wanted to go. When I make a decision that is it. I can't think about anything else other than just getting on with it. The thought of waiting it out until Friday was too much. Funny eh? Luckily one of my best friends and I had already booked a weekend away. It felt natural to continue on the journey from there. The campsite was on the way, so what was the point of going away and coming back? So... as soon as I finished work, I put my out of office on with no fixed return date and then was just about to clock off when one of the fellow analysts saw the holiday sign, panicked and asked for my mobile number. She said in justification 'If I have questions while you are away, I will need to contact you.'

Erm bollocks to that! Sort your own shit out! Selfish? Probably... The point of going away was not to work. So I was polite and said, 'I am going off-grid in my van. I will be switching off my phone and won't be available. That is the point of this trip – to take a proper break and completely switch off from work. I am sure one of the other analysts will be able to help.'

'I guess you haven't heard. Five of the analysts have been kicked out of the door today. It means that you and I are the only ones left. I guess they didn't mention it because they knew you were going on your trip. Sorry I didn't mean to be the bearer of bad news.'

How do you respond to that? Five analysts had been chopped by lunchtime. They had been informed that morning and were out of the door within the hour. That was a side-winder of a surprise. All of their access would be revoked and they would essentially not exist by midday. They would have been given two month's pay and whatever they were working on would not be complete. It wasn't my problem. The powers that be had made their decisions and knew I was going away. They still made the chop decision without a back-up plan. Half of me was stunned, the other half of me was honoured that they kept me, even though I was going off gali-van-ting for three months. The thing was that could just have easily been me. The problem was there was no one to cover my work. I took a deep breath. It wasn't my problem. I didn't need to 'save the day'.

Moments like that are the perfect reminder that you are doing the right thing. I read a quote that essentially said *'Why stay loyal and work your guts out for a company that can replace you in a second if you are unwell?'* I pondered what had happened. I decided I definitely would not be available during the trip. If a company could treat people like that then I could be kicked out of the door on my return. Luckily I had the financial reserve in place – should that happen.

I said my goodbyes to my colleague and then walked around my flat. I unintentionally picked up a bag and automatically filled it with 'just in case items'. In the last moments leading to departure I fell into bad habits. I realised I was going to take the bag and who knows... I might be glad that I had a deformed cake cover decorated with daisies.

CHAPTER 15

DICK EVASION TECHNIQUES

Now, what I will say is there are people within the vanning community who view others on the campsites as sitting ducks to share their woes, their wonders or their weirdness. There is a definite need to learn discernment, who to chat to, who to be amicable with and who to definitely avoid. Sometimes people forget others are on holiday to get away. On this particular little jaunt I had arranged to meet one of my great friends. She doesn't have a van, so we selected a place where she could glamp and I could van-it up. She liked the idea of the van life, but also knew it wasn't for her. She is always very honest and will say 'Oooooh no…'.

As I mentioned before, we had arranged to meet at the location because of our different work schedules. She wanted to head over early, after she had finished with her morning clients. I finished at five-thirty and had selected the location because it was just over an hour from where we lived, beside Monkey World and close enough to some brilliant village names like Slap Bottom, Happy Bottom and Shitterton. I know! Absolutely epic in terms of potential for pictures beside signage.

Anyway, I rocked up to the campsite and parked at my allocated electrical hook-up. Beside me was a large mobile home. It was huge, had a satellite dish and could easily be a residence. It turned out that I was right because the 'resident' emerged and called 'Hello neighbour'. He seemed relatively sprightly, in his late sixties wearing wellies and a peak cap. He trotted over like a plucky chicken and announced, 'I've had good news today...' That is a clever 'hooking' line. I have to admit I was not in the mood. I wanted to see my pal and when he trotted over my gut flipped in an 'uh ohhhh' kind of way. Still I indulged him out of politeness. 'Oh good,' I replied.

'My cancer hasn't spread...'

Yes that was good news for him; however, it meant a lengthy onslaught about his ten year battle against cancer, how his wife had kicked him out and he now lived in his van. It was quite a monologue. I noticed my friend strolling down the path towards us and watched her grind to a halt. She had a very strong intuition and could tell that I needed saving. It seemed she was considering her best approach. She turned around, took a deep breath and adjusted her purple paisley wellies. She then ran down the path and called out to me. 'Quick I need your help. One of the alpacas has gone ballistic.' She then grabbed me and dragged me off. She called over her shoulder 'Terribly sorry but this is an alpaca emergency!' She then ran in the direction of her glamping pod with me in hot pursuit. We paused at the top of the hill and two boys in camouflage and a large fake bazooka trampled past and shot us. 'You're dead' the eldest called, who could not have been older than ten.

How do you respond to that?

'Oh I have been shot numerous times by those two youngens,' she said. 'Earlier they were hiding in the hedge with binoculars and reporting back to HQ.'

'By the way thanks for the save,' I said.

'Ah it turns out he has a bit of a reputation. You can move your van if you like. He seeks out the single women, gives them his sob story and then invites them for a drink. They are usually polite and agree.' My friend said.

'How do you know that?' I asked.

'I was chatting to the woman in the shop. What made it better is his name is Dick,' Vanessa grinned at me.

'What about the escapee alpaca?' I asked glancing across at an alpaca field. A cluster of calm alpacas chewed their food with their rather randomly wonky teeth. Their fringes reminded me of those lovely eighties hairstyles.

'Ah I didn't say they escaped, I said gone ballistic and in a sense they had because the camouflage chappies had been emulating firing ballistic missiles at them. So it wasn't actually a lie, more of an elaboration on an imagined circumstance,' she replied thoughtfully.

How often do you hear such a justification?

Anyway, Vanessa didn't seem her usual self. She was usually super energetic – to give you an idea she is in her late fifties and looks thirty-five. She runs long distances, can drink gin like no other, has never had a gin induced hangover and… she sleeps around four hours per night, which is why we don't share rooms anymore. Although we have been away sailing previously and she was happy to party all night for three nights in a row with only a couple of hours sleep. She wiped the floor with those in their mid-twenties, danced on the table and then proceeded to 'bundle' everyone who was sleeping in the main sailing cabin. She is utterly hilarious and works as a therapist. How she stays so cheerful with some of the gruesome things she has to deal with is beyond me. Both of us have a respect for each other's professions because neither could do what the other does.

Anyway, we sat on the veranda and watched the alpacas contentedly chew. We could faintly hear the whooping of the monkey's from Monkey World. Beyond the alpaca field there were old oaks, pine trees and beeches. The air was warm and that evening the light grew increasingly golden. I could feel my body relax, but Vanessa still didn't feel right.

'What's going on?' I asked. 'You seem out of sorts.'

'Ah I don't want to burden you…' she said.

'Well you can't give a response like that and think there is no burden…' I replied with a shake of my head.

She smiled. We have been friends for over twelve years and met when we had Network Spinal Analysis – a kind of Chiropracting. The moment we met, we simply bonded and have been great friends ever since. We read each other, listen to each other and completely understand each other.

She shook her head sadly and made a loud sigh. 'I am so glad we are out here… So basically one of my friends was having a few issues with her vision. When she went to the doctors they booked her an MRI scan. It turned out she had a huge brain tumour. Her system was riddled with cancer, it was already in her bones.' There was a crack in Vanessa's tone.

'Surely they could do something…' I said.

Vanessa sighed and scratched her cheek. 'No it's incurable. They gave her a couple of months to live. She is only forty-four. What makes it worse is she lives a healthy lifestyle, doesn't drink or smoke. She isn't married, hasn't got any children and basically has two months left on the planet – if she is lucky. Anyway, she came over this morning and I stepped into professional mode. If you have two months left, suddenly everything becomes irrelevant. So we came up with a plan and a list of everything she wanted to experience before 'departure'.

'Gosh,' was all I could say. I was mid-forties and the thought of having such catastrophic news at that age was terrifying. 'So what did she come up with?'

'I think this is what upset me the most. Nothing spectacular. If she could do anything, experience anything then surely there would be some exciting things. All she really wanted at that point was a spa day,' Vanessa replied.

So two months left on the planet and she desired one spa day before departure. She must have been in shock. Spas are nice but two months... Bloody hell – you could really experience in that time. Talk about a kick up the arse! It then occurred to me that the poor woman was probably exhausted, shocked and just wanted some pampering to process the reality of what she had been told.

Vanessa made a huge sigh. 'Well that was where it began. We managed to shift her mind-set – she was pre-occupied with what she could afford. I had to provide a reality check about death. I realised she was in shock and going through the motions. It is amazing what the mind does to protect your from the acceptance of your own demise. So I said, imagine you sold your house, because there is no one to inherit it from you, and you had all of that money. Then what would you do?'

Imagine that - all of that disposable income, a limited time on the planet and unlimited possibility. I wondered what I would do and... strangely it was precisely what I was doing. I would go on a lovely adVANture to all the most beautiful and remote places around the U.K. Why the U.K when there was the whole world? Well I had been around the world eight times when I worked on cruise ships – I wanted a different experience, one with forests and nature - one that did not remind me of work. Of course lots of people would go on a cruise and numerous times I have met people who were terminally ill who would take a world cruise knowing there was a hospital on board and that if they died there was a morgue. I always found it fascinating how we are designed to be complacent about life and avoid the reality of our own deaths, as though it only happened to other people.

Well Vanessa's friend had the full body realisation that she was going to die and she could not avoid that truth. Vanessa held space for her as the full comprehension unravelled. Rage, anger, upset, sadness, resentment and grief were just a few of the emotions that erupted during that session. The pair then reviewed her 'spa day' and actually fell about laughing when that was all she had considered to experiencing. They then re-focused on what she would really like to experience in two months, bearing in mind the last month she was likely to rapidly decline.

Now, at this point, quite a few people would become angry. They would suggest that this woman should fight the cancer rather than accept the diagnosis. The thing was in the pit of her being she had known that something was up and she didn't want to 'fight' and be a 'martyr'. She desired to live the limited time she had left well. That was why she went to Vanessa. So what did she come up with? She wanted to fly in a private jet. Go for a jaunt in a gyrocopter. A gong bath experience. A track day with her mum. A few spa days with her mum in an exclusive hotel. A paddle boarding adventure, a laughter day and a tantric massage. That was in the first month of living before death. She would then see how she felt and if she had the energy for any more or if anything had changed in the diagnosis.

The pair of us sat in silence for a while gazing out at the landscape.

'How are you feeling?' I asked.

'A bit depleted, to be honest. It also makes you realise that can happen to anyone at any time. It makes me wonder whether I am living my life well and truly enjoying it. If not what do I need to change? It also makes you consider who is in your life. Who is draining and who is energising? It made me contemplate what more can I experience? I have been caught up in work and taking on more and more clients to help people. It seems I might have been consumed in helping others rather than considering and rejuvenating myself. That is why I am so pleased we are out here. I really needed a change of scenery. I need some head space to think… Plus it is always good to have a 'rubber ducky'.

For those that don't know – a rubber ducky is a techy term. When we (techies and developers) are figuring out a problem, we often work alone. To figure out a problem one needs a sounding board. The thing is most techies (who are geeky) often work odd hours, meaning they like to work through the night. So, finding a sounding board at three in the morning is a bit of a task. So, many of them have a rubber duck that they talk to. Yes, it might sound weird. They talk the problem aloud to the rubber duck, which often provides a solution. What I mean is by talking the problem out loud the developer finds the solution rather than the rubber duck quacking a response back. I told Vanessa about the concept and she loved the idea of the rubber duck. So what she did was invest in a giant rubber duck and put it in her 'counselling cabin' to 'rubber duck it up' when there was a difficult sequence of events to process. The client could talk to the giant rubber duck while she observed. It might sound eccentric but it worked.

'So what are you thinking?' I asked.

'Well I am trying to work out what I want to experience more of.' Vanessa replied thoughtfully.

'Okay…'

She looked at me intensely, 'What do you want to experience more of?'

'Laughter, fun, nature, adventure, spas, ease, health, vibrancy, kindness, family, friendship and connectedness,' I replied in a matter of fact tone.

'Just like that… You come up with it just like that…' she said shaking her head. 'Have you been thinking about this then?'

'Nope… I just think those are the things I value the most. Plus I am on an adVANture and my mind space has been freed up from huge system architectures. There is space in the mental warehouse,' I replied and decided that I might actually have a fruit cider.

Vanessa did her right-eyed squint, which revealed she was reading me. 'Okay what's going on?'

I could never get away with it.

'Something has happened hasn't it?'

Talk about busted. 'It isn't really something happened, it is more that I can't believe what my company has done. I was just putting my out of office on when one of the other analysts asked for my number so she could contact me while I was away. I essentially said no.'

'That is perfectly normal to say no while you are on holiday,' she said with a curious expression as she tried to figure out where the conversation was going.

'Well it turns out that the company kicked out five of the analysts today and that only leaves her to do all of the work while I am away. That means there is no one to cover my work. Plus the way the company is so brutal. You are working on something and are completely focused. The next moment you are called by H.R and you are out of the door. Boom! Gone! Just like that! I just find it upsetting how ruthless a company can be and how it can treat people.'

Vanessa was quiet as she contemplated the set of events. 'What arseholes and what idiots. So there is one person to do six people's work? Well good luck to them. No doubt the last one standing will be off with stress. So whatever happens, don't answer the phone to work. This is your trip, your life and it was agreed. Ahhhh now I get it... You were churning it on your way over weren't you?' She said. She knew me too well.

'Yep, full mental churn and numerous 'what if' scenarios. What if they make me redundant while I am away...? What if they ask me to come back half way through? My mind then traversed into what would I do... what do I like doing and what a bunch of wankers to do that the day I am leaving to go and live life to the full.' She pointed at the alpacas.

Vanessa smirked and sipped her gin, 'What a day for us both... and... now we are here just chilling out and enjoying. What a lucky pair we are... I have a gin, you have a fruity cider, let's make a fire-pit and have some sausages, baked veg and pickle. Oh and we have desert. I brought cheesecake. What more could you want?'

'Right we need to get the wood from the van and the fire-pit, and that means facing Dick,' I said.

Just as we said that, we noticed the hedge near us rustle and the two camouflaged kids crawled on their stomachs past the glamping pod. 'We have the perpetrators in sight...' they said as they crawled past.

'They are here for the tank museum,' said Vanessa. 'I met them earlier, they freed me from potential hostage taking when I ran into Dick. I owe them and am very happy for them to scope out the area and seal it off from potential Dick perpetrators,' she said.

We headed back to the van via reception and requested to move spots. Luckily I hadn't fully set up and there was a hook-up at the other end of the field which was concealed by another large mobile home. This time it was an auto-cruiser. It was large enough to hide Blossom and high enough to block any winds. What's more, the way it had been set up with awnings and wind breakers meant that I would have a level of privacy because the couple in that van clearly demonstrated that was what they wanted for themselves. Perfect!

That evening we sat gazing at the fire and the stars. It was a half moon and the temperature wasn't too terrible. There are times when I have sat out and gradually seized up as the cold crept into my bones. There is nothing like a good blanket and my blanketed hooded garment has become my 'go to'. I won't mention brand names, but the hooded blanket is a really cosy hit with many campers. A vaneer can sit out in the cold encapsulated by an oversized hooded garment and not freeze to death. What I love about such evenings and great friends is you can sit silently and just stare into space for a bit, have a chat and then stare into space some more.

The air grew increasingly crisp and an iridescent halo surrounded the moon. It was going to get cold. Vanessa had a good sleeping bag, but I wondered whether the temperature was going to drop down below zero. I had noticed that year that pre-dawn was particularly cold, even in April. Quite often it was minus two or worse. Many times Blossom's inner screen had ice coating it rather than condensation.

That evening we talked a lot about what we wanted to experience more of in life. It all came down to play, laughter, love and fun. Oh and to do things with ease rather than struggle. How do you enjoy more rather than strive? We wondered. We talked about conditioning, our unconscious patterns and why we always wanted more when simplicity seemed to be the key. Also we both realised how we fill our lives up so we can always do more and 'fit it in'. We both spent a lot of our lives on social treadmills. It was funny how we came to the same conclusions, although, where we differed was Blossom and van life. Vanessa would not want to adVANture, instead she would rather do a tour with nice hotels. She also said that she would not want to be away from friends and family for so long or go alone. That was where I am comfortable. I love taking myself off to random places and experiencing them alone. As much as the start of the trip had a few of my friends joining me, the further away I went then the fewer people I knew would be joining me. That would mean I would have proper space to recharge.

Talking of sleeping: there have been times when I end up completely twisted in the sleeping bag. Oh and another thing I learned is what to wear in bed, it is definitely worth having pyjamas that are cosy and soft plus thermal socks. Thermal hats are worth considering too although if I don't have to wear one I won't.

At ten-thirty I boiled the kettle and filled my two hot water bottles. One for the bottom of the sleeping bag and one for the middle. I really cannot sing the praises of hot water bottles enough. The thing is with a sleeping bag one usually uses their body heat to warm the 'bag', so, if you are already cold it takes time. I have a double square sleeping bag because I like space and can't bear being limited in leg movement. Not that I need to do the can can in my sleep. I just like a bit of free motion and don't like feeling confined. We all have our 'things'. The hot water bottles quickly heat up the sleeping bag and heat the gaps that often form between the bag and the body when sleeping on one's side. Who would have thought that even the general sleeping bag gapage would be analysed and solutionised. So ultimately a hot water bottle is brilliant! I LOVE HOT WATER BOTTLES!

By ten-thirty in the evening I was done, my early morning rise due to the traffic noise outside my flat had become ingrained. I always thought it was my bio-rhythm; however, when I started sleeping until eight in the morning on van trips, I realised something else was a-foot. The traffic noise begins at five-ish and starts to calm around ten. It seemed that I was unconsciously aware of that and had tailored my behaviour accordingly.

I will be honest, I do sleep better in the van than in the flat and actually wake up refreshed. I do generally have to pee in the night which means getting out of a cosy sleeping bag and baring a bottom to a porta loo in the cold. Yet I seem to instantly fall asleep once I climb back into bed.

Before bed Vanessa gave me a tour of her glamping hut and we sat on her mini veranda. The hut was called Daisy, she had chosen it because it had the same name as her bright yellow car. Across from the hut the alpacas were settling down, preparing for slumber. I meandered back to Blossom reflecting on our conversations. That night had provided a very real perspective on life and had evidenced that I was doing the right thing by living my best life now

CHAPTER 16

WHOOPING LOVELY

I woke up to sunrise which was a red glow, and had my coffee and dark chocolate. I sat on my fold-out chair and listened to the monkey's whooping in the distance and watched the early morning mist hover around the nearby trees. When you wake up to such wonder it is a joy to be up and living your best life. There is no alarm, just a natural desire to get up and feel that new day.

At eight in the morning Vanessa wandered over and was full of beans. Literally. She had had baked beans and was bounding along like someone who needed to expel excess energy or gas. It seemed she had slept well, had a huge cup of tea on her veranda and was ready to go for a long walk. She had already showered and was ready for the day... She actually felt refreshed. I cooked us breakfast (her second) and we sat just taking it all in. No rush, and a view of alpacas and their random hair dos. To our right two hedges started to move, dropped to the ground and crawled in the direction of our breakfast. That was enough for me to go and take a shower and prepare for a walking adventure. One of the jokes Vanessa and I have is that she has no sense of direction. We say we will go for a stroll and thirteen miles later we are still attempting to find our way back to the car or van. One simple bike ride found us in a swamp wading through with our bikes being carried above our heads.

What makes these sequence of events so strange is that they always happen, so much so that in my mind, when she says three miles, I multiply it by five and allow a day for any adventure because we have to consider returning from 'lostness'. On this particular day we decided to have a stroll around Wareham Forest. A pine tree filled forest is a very relaxing and a nice stroll. We took food with us, this is another learning because being lost without food and drinks is far worse than being able to have a little picnic whilst trying to figure out where you are.

Now imagine this, we actually followed a path for a while, until my friend got bored of being normal, and I noticed she instinctively increased her speed and headed towards a small path the led into the trees. 'Ermm… I can see what you are up to…'

She paused, 'I can't get away with it with you…'

The thing is the getting lost technique is this – your friend notices a path less travelled and feels the desire to explore. They walk definitely in that direction and people follow because the walking is definite and would suggest that she knows where she is going. I have known her long enough to know she has no clue and that there is a pattern to being stuck in a remote place with no idea where you are, or which direction will take you home, because the places usually don't have access to Wi-Fi or mobile networks.

I have to admit I indulged her because we didn't have to be anywhere, we had food and there was no time limit. So off we go into the depths of tree wilderness and ended up in a little valley area filled with butterflies. We sat on a mossy tree stump and just watched butterflies flitting around. It was lovely. A couple of woodpeckers pecked in the trees above and we saw a couple of jays. It felt wonderful. We had a snack and a drink and continued through until we found a boggy area. There were mounds of more solid grass in the boggy area so we went bog hopping. It was hilarious. If you go fast enough the bog lumps don't sink. So we bog hopped to the other side, and emerged from the trees to find an obvious path. A few people with bikes and baskets were having a break and looking at a map. In the baskets each had a pup. They glanced at the map and glanced at us to ask directions. My friend laughed when she was asked and explained that we had no clue where we were or the direction back. She was right... We had no sense of where we were but I had noted the direction of the sun and some pivotal points on nearby hills. I always do that now when I am with her because we went on a trip in Sri Lanka and she said she was much better at navigating cities. She wasn't. I let her think she was taking us back to the hotel and noticed that she picked the turning that went in the opposite direction that would have led us out of the city. I politely told her that her selection would result in not going where we wanted and she found it hilarious and allowed me to take us back to the hotel without ending up in a run-down area of the city...

Anyway I have story deviated in the same way as we path deviated. Well, we ended up walking for three more hours making it a total of around six by that point and I suggested that we started heading back. She laughed once more, 'I thought we were heading back.' I shook my head – 'We are going in the opposite direction. We need to be going that way… '

'Ooops'.

'What I like about you is that you never get upset or angry about the deviations. Some of our other friends have cried, gone ballistic or had complete meltdowns.'

'Ah that is because they don't plan to walk for at least eight hours when you say two…'

With that in mind, we followed an obvious path back and every time she felt the need to explore I reined her in…

We arrived back at the site at around six-thirty in the evening, when we had set out around ten for just a couple of hours…

She checked her feet and they were blistered… She had cooling cream with her, so applied that and I prepared the fire pit for another fatty sausage bonanza.

Across the field the young hedges were ambushing unsuspecting new arrivals. Unfortunately they weren't so accommodating as my friend and I, and told them to 'get lost' beginning with 'F'. Not very nice to tell a child. Anyway we cooked our tea and sat with our drinks, watching the alpacas. I literally love alpaca hairstyles and their teeth. I wonder what they must make of each other... Anyway we were both tired and I wasn't thinking when I picked up the loop of the top of the fire pit and burned my fingers... I had a special glove to do it and through tiredness forgot that it would be hot. My friend went and grabbed her cooling cream and plasters and we wrapped my fingers up. Talk about huge blisters. I will be honest, I am not the kind of person who will make a big thing about such an event but it is worth noting that one always needs a first aid kit for the van. You never know when you will get bitten, burned or cut. My friend was more concerned than I was... I just shrugged, it happens... You get on with it... I wasn't going to let burned fingers and a thumb ruin things. So I had a rhubarb gin and tonic. We sat and took in the evening sunset, which was spectacular. The sky turned red and an apocalyptic vision of a dark sun sunk below the tree horizon... The moon rose and the temperature fell. I put the fairy lights on, laid in my hammock and chatted to my buddy about life and our plans for the future. We talked some more about her friend with two months to live. We delved into what we would really want to see and do with such limited time. It was odd how such a sorry state of affairs had made us both delve deep into our lives. As much as the catalyst was painful it became a chance to re-evaluate. In the end we had a wonderful shared experience... Even though both of our legs might have been a little tired and when we looked at our step count it seemed we had walked fifteen miles... We had intended to do five at the most.

CHAPTER 17

BEING A SINGLE WOMAN

That night I laid in bed thinking about the woman having to face her demise. I really felt for her. It definitely put things in perspective. I thought about life and what was the true purpose? That little voice whispered, 'To truly know yourself and what you are capable of'. I liked that little voice. So many people believed in 'finding love, chasing ideals or being successful'. Does that really matter if you have two months left on the planet? If I had two months left would I contact Ryan? I laid thinking about it. I then wondered whether I would want to meet someone while on such a travel. That took me into a thought spiral about being single and the virtues of it.

After meeting Dick with his 'hook approach' and all of my relationship dramas over the previous years, I decided to have a break. Why water dead plants when you should be watering yourself? It is very easy to get caught up in relationships and chasing the next one in the hope to find 'the one'. I will be honest, I never bought into Hollywood ideals; however, I wanted to do the big adVANture with me and for me. What is funny is that I half expected to meet other singles with vans on the way round. I assumed I would meet both male and female vaneers taking the opportunity for adventure.

As I said, that is what I expected. What I have found in the past few years of having a van is that single women are more likely to adventure in vans. I literally have only met a handful of men in vans going on trips alone. When there are chaps they are usually in a group. I hardly ever see a single chap rock up in his van, set up and then chill out. I could not tell you why that is. Maybe they are there but invisible. Maybe they wear camouflage. Of course there are groups of women in vans too (including myself). I have been away with my pals. I sometimes meet other women who are lone in a van but I have only met a few single chaps – one emerged from a hedge wielding an antler, another tried to convince me of the virtues of his two hundred foot hose and then there was Dick. Maybe it is because I don't tour the sites looking to see who is single and who is not. The thing is on sites people do watch and they do gage. Also, and this is something I completely don't get, when you are a single woman you often get adopted by couples. Not in a swinging sense. It is as if they feel sorry for you. Numerous times couples have come over for a chat to make sure I am 'okay'. It is really sweet of them and they often invite me for drinks. Maybe it is 'a bored couple' rescue thing. If we invite a singleton for drinks then they don't have to sit silently with each other. Or maybe it is out of genuine kindness that they come over to say hello and check in. Admittedly my van is a 'tiddler' among vans and people are curious about other people's vans and their layouts. When you have a van there is always a conversation or a van-versation. The amount of people who have asked to look inside my van because it is essentially a converted people carrier. I don't think the mobile homers, with their large interiors, can fathom how someone can reside in such a tiddler. When I do show them, many are amazed and the wife often comments that the bed would not be large enough for the pair of them.

Anyway, back to being single in a van. So many of my friends have said in jest that the reason I have a van is to pull a chap with a van. Again, it couldn't be further from the truth. As I said, I haven't seen many on campsites, which means maybe they are wild camping... That could be it - that could be where they are... Or they are all at surf breaks doing activities... Hmmm.

So the reason I write the bit about being a single woman, is that so many women fear being alone, or being judged for being alone. Well, I have tried being anti-social with a van and failed dismally. In the end I accepted that if I have a van then I will end up chatting to people. That is just how it is. If you want to be anti-social then wild camp, although that has not proven terribly successful because every time I have wild camped, I have managed to attract a number of other vans and it has turned into a party!

What advice would I give any single ladies who are somewhat fearful about AdVANturing alone? Dooooo it! What is the worst that can happen? You can spend three months alone and then get eaten by wolves that have escaped from a nearby zoo. That isn't likely. The thing is you never know who you will meet, or what you will experience. The point is though, you get to discover you, and what is possible with and for you. What if you take three months out and have a shyte time? Well you learned it isn't for you. The thing is we spend so much time doom-saying when actually what if it goes right? What if you have the most fantastic time and meet marvellous people and the wolves don't escape from the zoo? You would never know... What if you came from the angle of love rather than fear? What if you were amazed by life and were curious about all the wonderful places you could experience? There is so much potentiality, yet we often talk ourselves out of experiencing and enjoying by finding the reasons why not, rather than the reasons why. So what if you are single? So what if there are lots of couples on sites? We are all human and everyone has a story... So bollocks... Just do it!

That evening Vanessa and I made burgers on the barbecue and discussed relationships...

The following morning Vanessa and I took a little stroll because we both managed to lie in until at least eight. We wandered around the campsite, admired the alpacas and listened to the whooping of monkeys. Two nights away from normality had recharged Vanessa. It was just what she needed. Life had been put in perspective and she knew her course of action because she had clarity.

At ten in the morning Vanessa and I had a huge hug. Within the following month it was likely her friend would die. Such a short amount of time. *'When time starts running out... you will always want more. So never take it for-granted'*, came the inner whisper. Time running out was an odd concept. Such a dramatic turn of events had a huge knock-on effect. Our walking conversations had narrowed down what we wished to experience more of and who we wanted to spend time with. The future glowed with anticipation. My journey would more than likely change me and when I returned it would be interesting to hear how Vanessa had implemented her changes and whether she had experienced more of what she desired.

'Well you have fun!' she said as she climbed into her bright yellow car, grinned and waved as she departed.

I climbed into Blossom. That was already the first site on my adventure done. Just like that. Thank goodness there were so many more to experience.

CHAPTER 18

YOU ARE NEVER LOST UNLESS YOU ARE LOST

I didn't have far to drive. It would have taken most people around thirty minutes; however, it took me an hour because I spent thirty minutes being lost, or as Vanessa said, I was exploring other unintended avenues close to a location that I hoped to arrive at eventually.

Well, the top of the hill campsite provided astounding views in different directions. On one side Eype, with its undulating cliffs and sheer rock faces, and on the other side West Bay with glowing green grassy fields and bay views. On that particular morning the beauty of a rising sun and mysterious clouds suspended over green valleys, made one inhale in awe.

The campsite itself was so well run, had numerous pitches and a huge mobile home/campervan capacity. The pitches were on a first-come-first-served basis so there was definitely potential for public wrestling and prime-pitch-man/womanship. The prime-pitch thing is rather amusing because of the different ways people mark their territory: colourful windbreaks, different posts, elaborate dragon or fish wind socks, or the equivalent to washing lines with colourful sheets hanging from them. I have also seen displays of large knickers pegged to bunting. Flag... huge knickers... flag... arrangements. My favourite was a barricade made of garden gnomes all asserting the boundaries. It seemed the bunting and windbreaks were the defence option of choice, although that all became useless the moment a storm rolled in. That night there was a huge storm forecast and being at the pinnacle of a huge hill with no shelter certainly was going to make for some shaky shaky.

As mentioned before, the site is very well run and the wardens made their rounds. They informed all of the vaneers that a storm was due. All awnings had to be retracted, pop-tops were advised to be flattened and anything that could blow away was to be either taken down or pegged down. Could you imagine in the middle of the night your pop-top being ripped from your van when a seventy mile an hour gust ravished your vehicle?

Something a lot of people don't often consider is that when a storm is due, and one can determine which direction the wind is going to come from, it is worth simply turning your van into the wind. Think about it… Your van is designed to be aero-dynamic and travel along the road at seventy miles an hour. It has to be aerodynamic. Although, I do know plenty of people who may well reach higher van velocities and luckily their van is equally shaped to cope with ninety miles an hour. So, turning the van into the wind is a sensible option unless the wind is changeable. Being buffeted from the side is what makes the van feel like a ship riding huge waves.

With all of the above in mind, the pitch participants arranged their vans to face into the storm. Some sat and watched the ominous unfolding out to sea. I did wonder whether we would have lightening as well, which in itself would have been a greater concern because lightening is drawn to the highest pinnacle in an area. Admittedly there were some vast vans and massive mo-homes either side of me, which gave me a sense of comfort. Some had satellite dishes and huge antenna, which was most likely to attract anything electrical. I certainly had never considered what it would be like to be hit by lightning in Blossom. Such thoughts sent my mind into another mental churn. I will be honest, one of my big concerns about the trip was that I am very used to working long hours, problem solving and working with analytics. I am incredibly 'mental'. (Ha that made me smile) I was concerned my mind would get working withdrawal because when do you ever take three months off? When do you get a chance to completely re-charge? I am in my mid-forties and have worked since I was fourteen, so for over thirty-four years I have worked and worked without taking a large stint of time off. I wondered what would happen during discombobulation... Would I become stupid without the constant mental stimulation or crave problems to solve? Did I need to play Sudoku? Maybe I would enjoy the mental percolation and processing. Maybe I would stimulate my mind in different ways. STOP!

I doubt many people would believe it was possible to over think overthinking. That was the challenge, being able to switch off and not think about work. It was weird really, how our lives are filled with so many hours working that it becomes our normal. Of course work provides purpose and income, but what do you do when you actually have space to go slowly? My gut said the 'space fills'. You fill that space with other things. It is a rule of physics.

So, after a little mental detour, I set up my chair in front of my van and watched the storm building out to sea. At first there were a few clouds, which miraculously attracted others. It was as if a whole storm front unfurled before our eyes. Now the reason I say 'our' is because my van-neighbours – vanbours followed viewing suit. They set up their fold-away chairs, cracked open some beers on one side, and gin and tonics on the other. The beer drinkers were Alf and Roberta, mid-sixties – they were retired. He was a grinning baldy with a beer bump. He had run a building firm, and she was a glamorous blonde with a cockney accent and her own mobile hairdressing business. They had a fat pug called Burt, who was constantly sniffing around for anything he could nibble. He was quite a character because he had huge 'feed-me' eyes. If you had food he would trample over and sit in front of you grunting. His sad eyes would be off-set with drool tendrils. I think it was a double-pronged food attack. If the sad eyes didn't get you then he would shake his head. Drool would fly through the air and spatter you. He was cute and wore a red bandana around his neck which made me think of bandits. Alf and Roberta were regulars at the site because it was dog friendly and had a dog food menu. A pup could feast on a doggy roast or have a three dog sausage meal and dog ice-cream for desert. Burt loved the place and there was even a dog exercising field where Burt would stomp down to the middle of the field, ignore his ball, have a sniff around and then sit looking at the view.

The gin drinkers on the other side were two buxom cheerful ladies in their late fifties who definitely had a thing for knitwear, woolly hats and obscurely patterned Wellington boots. After a conversation about the large knicker deterrent technique, they erected a large knicker display and secured them in such a way those knickers were storm resilient. They had special gin glasses – one said 'Gin-a-ling-a-gin-dong' and the other said 'A gincident waiting to happen.' Gloria and Betty were hilarious, they had loud raucous laughs and were extremely excited by the storm. Of course a conversation about a storm evolved into a bit of a life story/confession. That's what happens with van life, people are friendly, open and often summarised their life story in the first ten minutes of meeting them.

Gloria and Betty had once been married to male spouses, both had had children, both had been divorced and both had 'switched sides', as they described it. That was all confessed in the first ten minutes of knowing them and they were on their third gin. I had a hot chocolate (extreme - I know).

When we first set up our chairs there was a bit of a spiralling breeze. It felt as though it was searching out the storm's destination by 'scoping out the joint'. It was the kind of breeze that gently lifted wisps of hair to tickle your nose. Anyway, that recognisance draft gained power as nature intensified her cloud density. I do find it amazing when a blue sky background cuts to a clear cloud edge. Then the angular vision of rain falling beneath the clouds creates a haze as it pounds the sea.

Well, we sat and watched the storm creep towards us. A water spout rose up from the sea and spun elegantly towards the land. It really was quite a spectacle. I sipped my hot chocolate, Betty and Gloria emptied the gin bottle into their glasses and went and found another while Burt did a rather rapturous dog blow-off and barked at his behind. Alf and Roberta laughed, 'It is as if he is telling his bottom off.'

I watched a random receipt blow past, the storm was most definitely gaining momentum.

There was a connection between the groups because we were united in a strange fascination with danger as the storm charged towards us. It was as if all the vaneers were wanting to play chicken with it, or see who would stay the longest before bolting into the comfort of their vans. Apparently that behaviour was normal because the site staff circled the pitches in their souped-up golf-cart vehicle. They suggested we pack up and get inside. What party poopers! Or storm-squashers. Of course we all did as we were told, which coincided with the storm surging. Within five minutes that tickling draft transformed into blustery, belting blasts. It was lucky we packed up when we did and went inside because it was as if a giant pair of hands decided to shake our vans. I will be honest, I actually found it quite relaxing. I know that is weird, but I spent years working on cruise ships and learned to sleep though the most intense storms. Sleeping in Blossom was like being in a cruise ship's cabin. The shaking was strangely comforting, some might say it is like the rocking of a crib, others might liken it to being in a blender. I guess it was the state of mind of a person at any given time.

Now the wind is one thing, but hailstones and huge downpours are another. Unfortunately I discovered I had a leak above the back window. I think it's where the reversing camera's wire cuts into the spoiler. The deluge of water resulted in a bit of a squirt running down the back window. I will be honest - I was peeved. I hadn't seen that happen before and the rain had just hit the end of my bed. In my wisdom I jammed some kitchen roll into it, which then created a larger gap for more water to run through. Bollocks! Oh and here we go... The mind decided we would have a flood through the night. I was not going to get into a mental battle of worst-case scenarios of drowning in bed then being hit by lightning. I put kitchen roll along the window, sealed it with gaffer tap and moved my pillows down a bit. Do I put on rubber wellington boots just in case? I was proud of myself because I made a very neat seal. I wondered how many people understood the joy of gaffer tape and kitchen roll. Both items are saviours in a van. Kitchen roll is really the ultimate necessity.

After the DIY, I laid on my stomach on my bed gazing out at the storm. I couldn't see much due to the rain, which turned into huge hailstones. It sounded like golf balls hitting the roof. What a noise! Half of me considered going to bed, but there was no way a person could sleep through the ping-ponging of hail as it hit Blossom's metal roof. In times like that it was best to simply curl up and read a book or get the portable DVD player out. I usually put on headphones because there was no way one would be able to hear much while Blossom was pounded by spherical sky ice. What I find fascinating is how in films, storms often calm down within a few hours. That one was rebellious and continued through the night, and most of the next day. I wasn't bothered to be honest. It was an excuse to not do much. I had food in the fridge, coffee and a small 12V coffee maker (which I love). There was nothing like waking up to a sunrise, and having an expresso with dark chocolate. You can charge the thing through the cigarette lighter, or use the 12V slot in the back of the van or plug into the hook-up. What makes that little gadget even better is that it charges up to enable the coffee addict up to three shots without having to find a power source. I know... amazing. There is nothing like a good bit of gadgetry. Of course one can simply boil the kettle on the stove and use a cafetiere – I have to admit that I unintentionally typed catheter then. Imagine if that little typo had stuck. Yes, I do actually use a catheter to make coffee – the mind boggles!

The storm gained force through the night. I slept deeply, yet was aware that the blustery blasts were belting us. I would not have wanted to leave Blossom through fear of blowing off – meaning the wind picking up a person rather than the intestinal passing sort. Talking of intestinal passing. Thank goodness I had a porta potty. What is good about having the van to myself is that I can 'contemplate my naval' whilst sitting on a porta potty. The starting thought begins with *why would anyone sit on a toilet contemplating their naval*? Then what is the point of contemplating a naval? Then… *Aren't navel's weird?* And so on… Had I still been in a relationship with Ryan, I think that porta potty usage for ones and twos would have most likely deflated any passion. Being stuck in a confined space with someone else's stink would be enough to generate all levels of hatred. I completely understand why couples invest in mobile homes with hot showers and a proper toilet. It solves two kind of stink issues – bodily stink and bottomy stink- which probably saves most relationships when on the road for any extended amount of time.

I did think about Ryan during the storm and what he would have made of the adventure. Admittedly I had a bit of a cry. I am glad I let it out. I was so disappointed, yet the sequence of events worked in my favour. If life hadn't taken that turn I wouldn't have 'Stuffed it!' In retrospect I think that the universe had provided a lucky escape and a reason to adventure. Maybe I am creating a story or a positive spin on a shyte situation, but the truth is, if I hadn't split up with Ryan I would not have been there. I did miss him and at times I felt really sad and disappointed. It really hurt to be lied to and then discover the horrible history behind the facade. I never understood how people could be so cruel. I came to the conclusion it wasn't for me to figure out. I desired a life without drama and filled with fun. If a person did not add any positivity to your life then they could piss off!

When the storm finally snaked off I burst out of my van in my polka dot wellies and polka dot poncho – imagine actually matching! I took a deep breath, grabbed a bottle of water and made my way down the hill to the Eype side of the campsite. There was still a strong breeze and the poncho flapped like a cape. One gust proved that a poncho could be lifted and form a tube that one had to wrestle down to be able to see. I must have looked like one of those dogs that had the see-through lampshades on their head embellished with polka dots. After a good bit of arm flapping I managed to gain control of the poncho and tucked it in my trousers. I then glanced about to see if anyone had seen. A chap sat in the front of his van crying with laughter. Fabulous! He wound down the window and through gasps of breath cried, 'That just made my day! That was epic! I could never have guessed such a random thing could happen!'

I smiled, I was glad I had entertained a random chap in a van with a bit of poncho wrestling! His wife entered the side door and shook her head in an *I can't believe what I just witnessed* way. 'That was phenomenal!' She said.

'I am glad it brought a smile to your face!' I replied feeling a bit of a knob.

The pair rubbed the tears from their eyes. 'It was brilliant!'

I waved and headed in the direction of the coastal path.

On the way I saw numerous privacy tents attached to trees and fence posts. Some of the vaneers had ignored the warning and numerous privacy tents had been shredded. I followed the footpath down to the beach and marvelled at how much driftwood had been thrown up from the sea. I stood by the sea and watched the huge waves crash. There was a moment of quiet and rumbling behind me. A chunk of cliff crashed down onto the beach. It was completely unstable. I had heard there were rockfalls in the area, but had not thought I would witness it. I have to say I felt vulnerable and did not intend to go near the cliff or by the edge when walking back. I wandered along the beach for around an hour and found some rather interesting rock formations and sat sipping my water. The trip had already been quite an adventure.

Admittedly, I purposely sat for a while because I was fighting the mental 'lunch hour or break syndrome'. Since my life was run by routine I have found that I have a tendency to limit my time doing things, as if I am on a break or lunch hour. I often felt as though I 'had to get on or get back'. I didn't realise I did that until I had a couple of days off work and fell into 'work routine'. I then noticed I had a tendency to divide my days at the weekends too. It was a bit of a shocker how timing habits had become my normal. Once I recognised it, I decided to change it. It was challenging because habits are about moving into a state where you don't have to think about something you just do it.

CHAPTER 19

WHEN FRIENDS INVITE THEMSELVES

The first part of the trip involved spending time with some of my buddies, which was nice. However, the point was to go and be with one's self. To see what one is capable of when they travel alone. So often the big question regarding trips is whether you go alone, with buddies or meet up with friends on the way. I have to admit that when I travel I am a bit of a lone wolf and often go away to get away from social engagements and the endless 'doing' treadmill. The truth is I am a socialised introvert. I like nothing better than being on my own in remote places – some people find that weird. As a survival mechanism I became very sociable and no one would ever know that I prefer complete aloneness to being with people. I like silence, solitude and nature.

Life never really delivers on aloneness because I have to work. I live in an area filled with people and I have an extremely busy social life. However, every so often I just have to completely step away, shut down and recharge. Obviously I like hanging out with friends in our vans because it provides a different experience – a shared experience. The thing is the adVANture was all about discovering what I was capable of and whether I really could endure reclusivity – I created that word to be exclusively reclusive. Unfortunately in the run up to my 'Big AdVANture' I became a little bit too excited and ended up talking about what I wanted to do along with the places I intended to visit.

On one occasion I mentioned to one of my fellow vaneers that I intended to go on an adVANture which would start relatively locally. Now that friend – Andrea- was a lovely lady, who is rather esoteric in her approach to life, well 'a bit wafty'. What's more, we are completely opposite in our circadian rhythms because I am an early bird and she is a night owl. When we have gone vanning together previously she and I didn't see that much of each other because she woke up at midday and I woke up around six. She ate late, drank late and would go to bed very late. Half of the time I expected to see her still up when I was waking up. The thing with that friend was she liked to do things with people and did not like to be alone. She also had a tendency to befriend an entire campsite, which is something she loves, and it generally evolved into a massive party with a lot of weed smoking. We are quite the opposite – although I often manage to meet lots of people without trying to. My body has no capacity for alcohol – one drink and I am everyone's and after a rather unfortunate incident in Amsterdam in my teens where I ate three pieces of 'Brownie' without being aware of what it contained – me and the 'world of weedyness' are not on good terms. So, in some ways it is fine to be away with her because I still have my space and am not encroached upon.

Anyway, a few weeks before departure I mentioned that I had selected a location near Bridport – a place I had wanted to visit for a long time. I mentioned it was on the coastal path and had access to some lovely beaches. It was the perfect place to warm up into an adVANture. In truth I was just excited to go and stay there. A couple of weeks before departure she asked me to send the link to the place I was staying to see if she would want to go there too. Well, a few days before departure she let me know she had booked to go and invited one of her friends – Joy - who I could hang out with because she got up early too, paddle boarded and did yoga. Really? I had to admit I was stunned because when I mentioned my trip I said I was 'hanging, was completely exhausted and needed to recharge'. I had no space for people or socialisation at the beginning because I just needed to rest. Unfortunately she had not heard that and was concerned about me being alone. It seems her issues had been projected onto me.

When I mentioned to her that I had intended to be alone, so I could rest, she completely did not hear what I said. Instead, she told me that her friend had recently bought a van and just needed to get started... You know when you are like Ffs! I let the situation brew for a bit and did not react instantly. Instead I considered whether I should 'accommodate' or how I should approach the situation.

In the end I called my friend up and said 'I will be honest... I did want to go on the trip alone. I wasn't planning on putting energy into anyone else other than me because to be quite frank I am a bit broken at the moment and I need to recharge. I recharge by being alone.'

My friend was mortified. She had thought I was just being brave and was going alone because I had no other choice. That was another projection because she knows I have plenty of friends. She was telling one of her friends about the location and what I was up to and saw a connection. She was an early bird, we both did yoga and we both paddled. She realised she had got the wrong end of the stick and said they could cancel. She would have cancelled but I sighed and thought about it. I had the chance to go it alone for months. So why not meet a new person, hang out with a friend and just make the most of the fact that my lovely friend had misconstrued my 'I want to be alone' for 'let's all go together!'

As I mentioned before – some people like to be alone and others assume you are just saying you want to be alone because they don't want to be alone. The irony is that this friend has on numerous occasions wanted to create a gathering of vaneers and no one was available, so she had to go alone. Which, is something she is learning to enjoy. It seems the universe was showing her the other end of the 'aloneness spectrum!'

In terms of going it alone or with buddies... Whichever suits your fancy. There is always the opportunity to meet people – if you want. Van-versations always take place and people love talking about their vans and their layouts. If you want to go alone – there are usually some remote or hidden pitches on site where you can make it clear you want solitude. It is just a matter of deciding why you are making the adVANture and what you want to gain/experience from it.

After staying by Eype for a couple more nights I actually took it slowly by not doing much other than taking a few walks, chatting to the sheep and reading my book. I made my way slowly, a whole twenty minutes down the road to my next site. My friend and her friend were going to arrive that evening.

CHAPTER 20

GOLDEN CAP

I arrived on site, checked the area for my friends and thought I would take the opportunity for a little explore before they arrived. I certainly had not anticipated how steep the hills were on either side of the Golden Cap, on the Jurassic Coast. When you consider taking a little stroll you don't expect to ascend a hill that makes your heart thump in your chest like a huge base drum. Now I am fit, I exercise every day; however, those hills are epic and certainly work muscles you never noticed.

Time to take a few steps back, excuse the pun… I decided to begin my epic adVANture with some sites that were close by and well serviced. As the trip went on I would grow more adventurous, rather than dropping myself in at the proverbial wild camping deep end. What's more, the friend of mine, who had decided to join me and had invited her friend, were glad of showers and toilets even though both could be self-contained.

Golden Cap site was an hour and a half from where I lived and there were plenty of other campsite opportunities in and around this area – Eype being the one I chose with the most astounding view. The thing that made this particular selection quite extraordinary was there was another huge storm forecast for the days we were going to be staying there. As mentioned, I am not bothered by storms because I spent a lot of years at sea; although, this particular storm had winds of over eighty miles an hour. The storms seemed to be upping their game. As a van newbie there were going to be testing conditions. In addition, my wafty friend was often quite fearful, tearful and emotional. I have to admit I was somewhat apprehensive. Plus I was staying on another open coastal site. How was that going to affect things? Would the storm roll off the sea, ravish us and then continue in land? How would my wafty friend deal with it? The mind went into yet another churn trying to consider all eventualities. In the end I came to the conclusion she would have to find her own way. What was the likelihood of having two huge storms so close to each other on a big trip?

Another thing I had not considered when driving a van was how cross winds really knock you sideways. I had noticed it in cars but not to the same extent. The wind had already picked up on the way to the site. Open areas along the dual carriageway provided a few shocking blasts. There were a few moments where I felt anxious because I would suddenly feel a gust shove me. I did wonder about my wafty friend, who had a tendency towards drama and was likely to scream every time the wind hit her mo-home. To make matters worse she had a high and long 1990s motorhome, which would definitely veer all over the road with the extreme gustage taking place. I actually felt for her. When we make our adVANture bookings we often have the brochure image in our mind rather than being tossed all over a dual carriageway with droves of rain cascading down the windscreen.

The friend of a friend had a smaller van and no doubt would be affected because she had not made any big drives yet. From what I could gather she was a roll with it kind of woman in her sixties. I had only met her twice; however, the couple of times I met her she seemed completely unphased by most eventuality and at peace. It was funny how we all had very different natures that resulted in completely different approaches and responses to the same situations. When things are testing I often switch into being very focused, very present and alert. On the way I noticed a caravan get blasted by a gust. The car driving it must have panicked when they noticed the caravan lift on one side. The car and caravan veered sideways. I guess the driver must have felt it and responded the best way they knew how.

Further down the road lorries pulled into to laybys because the wind was growing gnarly. I have seen pictures of trucks and lorries blown over before - it was likely the same could happen that day. After an hour I managed to drive off the open road into some narrow, sheltered lanes which led to the site where we were camping. I have to say it was a huge relief and my body relaxed. However when I arrived my friend, the highly strung one was already there and crying like an overwhelmed toddler. Bless her! She had been convinced she was going to die and was in a hugely emotional state. She shook with fear as she recounted the gusts that hit her side on. About half an hour later the 'roll with it' friend turned up completely unphased and climbed into my friend's van to be greeted by a sobbing mess. She gave her a cuddle, comforted her and said, 'Well you're alive, it is an adventure and now you can suck it up princess and enjoy yourself. This is life... Live it rather than fear it.'

I liked her attitude. I will be honest, I had been somewhat overcome by my friend's dramatic wailing display. I had calmed her; however, I was a little bemused by how emotional she was. She was shaking, crying and moving about erratically. I guessed she was very traumatised by the journey. She was now safe on the site but was still running mental churns of worst case scenarios and trees landing on her. Joy and I glanced at each other. I am pragmatic and analytical. Joy is peaceful and calm. Andrea was erratic, emotional and very fearful. It was quite a combination of traits. Although what I didn't expect was that I was only going to see Andrea for a few hours over the next few days. It was amazing what a combination of a storm, sleep deprivation and an opposing circadian rhythms can do to a person.

CHAPTER 21

BEING BENDY WITH A NEW FRIENDY

That following morning Joy and I met up and did yoga together. I had slept well and was feeling inspired. It was six-thirty in the morning. After that we did a breathing meditation and took a stroll down to the beach with her pup. It was a very easy interaction and just flowed. We talked about all manner of topic and the fact she had just purchased the van. Well she was not the newbie that Andrea had made her out to be. She was actually quite adept at vanning and had previously owned a mobile home and travelled across Europe when she was in her fifties. I didn't mention that Andrea had suggested that she was a newbie van driver.

After breakfast I took a stroll along the coastal path and up across the hills. I wanted some alone time and took a picnic. I made sure I slathered suntan lotion all over because the sun emerged after the storm and was pretty intense. I wandered up some very steep hills and found myself in a field full of cows. I do find cows concerning, especially when they don't have udders.

Luckily this faction of Friesians were not bothered by my presence. Once past the bovine beauties, I found myself mulling Andrea's fearful response to the drive in comparison to Joy's. It was strange how we all experienced the same situation and were affected differently. Well I found a few nicely positioned benches and had some water, contemplated, walked and then did the same again. There was no rush, just leisure. I saw a couple of rats, two mice and a number of kestrels. I only saw around six people and said hello to them. That was it.

At four in the afternoon I returned to the site and at four-thirty Andrea emerged from her van. That was equivalent to her morning. She had not slept all night because of the storm. Joy had trekked across the other hills nearby and had indulged in a cream tea.

Andrea had a coffee and we all went for a little stroll down to the beach together. She needed to get some pictures on location for two social media posts she made. We found some elaborate rock formations and I took some pictures for her. When we strolled back she seemed distant, consumed, and then I found out why. She was on a dating app and was chatting to a number of different chaps. It seemed that consumed her time. At six-ish Joy and I prepared our evening meals while Andrea ate her lunch. She was completely out of sorts, as if she was not present. She then talked about how she had been frightened during the night. All of her fears had played through her mind. Joy and I listened intently. Andrea was exhausted, she sighed and at eight o'clock went back to bed.

Joy and I set up our camp chairs, watched the sunset and talked about life, spirituality and the universe. We decided on an early morning Tai Chi sequence on a nearby hill.

By ten-thirty we went our separate ways and woke up at five-thirty. We cheerfully made our way to a beautiful spot overlooking the bay and did Tai Chi. The sea was still, the sun was warm, and sheep in nearby fields made themselves known in a harmony of 'baas'. Both of us lifted our energy and arrived at heightened states. When we were finished we glanced over at each other and gave each other a hug. Joy's pup sat contentedly chewing his bone. The fluff-ball with eyes made my womb convulse. I was most definitely puppy broody. I love dogs!

Neither of us had realised the time and when we returned to our vans we shockingly discovered it was close to nine in the morning. We made breakfast and sat cross-legged on the ground. I had cooked vegetables, avocado and eggs. She had a porridge with fruit creation.

At ten in the morning Andrea emerged from her van looking refreshed. She had slept all the way through. She glanced at her watch and screamed 'Shit!' She had an hour to pack up before departure. Essentially her little trip had been spent in her van and we had hardly seen her.

Joy told her what we had been up to and Andrea sighed. 'I knew you two would get on. I just can't believe what I missed out on. Thing is I have to go home because I have clients lined up.'

I felt for her because she really hadn't fully engaged with the place or her friends. She knew that and so did we. There was no point mentioning it, rather than an elephant in the room it was more of a hippo on the site.

CHAPTER 22

THAT RATTLING, AND RANDOM EVENTS

After spending a few more days exploring and venturing further along the coast it was time to move on. On my last full day I walked twenty miles. It was a little too far to be honest, so was glad to get in the van and move to the next location rather than walk again.

Well, one should never rush with a van. It is worth checking around the van, follow a checklist and make sure that everything is secured. There is nothing worse than going around a roundabout and all of your drawers flying open. Something I have learned before departing is to check the drawers and cupboards are locked and everything is where it should be. Some of the other vaneers I have met have a pre-drive checklist. There are many stories of people leaving in a rush. The level of regret that unfolded due to not making pre-departure checks was likened to arriving at the airport without a passport. As an example, there was a picture of a van that had forgotten to put its pop-top down and unfortunately proceeded to drive under a height restriction barrier. The image showed the pop-top contorted because the driver had continued, albeit there being resistance from above.

Another thing I make myself remember is to make sure I have switched off the gas. Admittedly most of the time it is safe to drive with the gas on, a lot of my friends have done it by accident and survived, but of course there will be that one time when something goes awry and you don't want to be the one who headlines in the paper after a random event which resulted in the side of the van being blown off.

Electrical hook-ups have to be detached. There have been numerous times where I luckily did a final check and saw that I had forgotten to detach the cable. You would only find out how strong that attachment between the points was by driving off. I wonder if anyone has ever dragged the electricity post out of the ground.

Of course there are the items that are left behind. I feel for whoever left their hammock and two fold-out chairs at one of the sites. I have seen pairs of shoes and wellies left behind, and the tracks that enable you to get out the mud.

You might do all of the checks and set off and then you have that rattle. There is something caught somewhere or trapped behind something. As you drive or go round corners the sound haunts you. You might try loud music or adjusting your driving strategy but whatever you do that rattle will remain until you face it because if you don't it will grate. On that particular journey something kept rolling and colliding. I could not be bothered to stop and had two hours of driving ahead of me. I would sort it out when I arrived at my destination. I knew that once I started searching it would result in an entire can of worms emerging and I may even have to pull everything apart. Unfortunately I had to listen to the blighter until I reached my destination. I knew that my shoulders would gradually rise and my jaw would grow taught with every corner, every bend and every roundabout.

About an hour into the journey, I turned the music up. I couldn't listen to whatever was rolling around anymore. The thing is I usually turn the music down or off when I come to an area that I feel challenged by. I don't know why but I always feel angsty when I have to drive via Exeter. I know that I am not the only one who has that same feeling. It isn't as if it is a long stretch, or that complicated, it is just that I always feel a sense of dread as I approach.

CHAPTER 23

DARTMOOR

Dartmoor was a natural choice on the way down to Cornwall and I had been drawn to the Haytor Rocks. There was something about them, they reminded me of sleeping giants. Admittedly I had considered going to North Devon to the Gnome Sanctuary, but unfortunately it had closed down.

I wondered whether that made me look bad in the eyes of the owner of the company. Although, in truth I doubt that he would think 'Well Ruby is going to a Gnome Sanctuary – I should look it up and see where she is retreating to.' Luckily I found there was actually another Gnome Sanctuary/Dell in Cornwall!

The journey to Dartmoor took me just over two hours because I thought I would take it easy. What I did not expect was how narrow the lanes were around the Haytor Rocks. What's more, there were only a few passing places along those tiny lanes. In the end I arrived by the Haytor Rocks at around four. I stopped at the visitor centre and scoped out the area. From what I had read, one could wild camp in Dartmoor. That meant I had to find a sensible location to park overnight. Admittedly there is an app that enables one to find locations and that was my first option.

The main rule with wild camping is to arrive late, leave early and leave no trace. I followed the app to a good location and considered my options. It seemed like a great place to stay overnight because it was on a plateau and had a wonderful view of the valley. Close to this layby area were plenty of walks and it was surrounded by trees, which meant the van was not obvious.

Once I had determined my sleeping location I decided to park up by the Haytor Rocks and take a walk. I was pretty stiff from the previous day's hike and driving in the van for a few hours had exacerbated it. I filled my thermos with liquorice tea and took a flapjack with me. I then took a little wander which evolved into a longer stroll than expected. I found a nice area of stones and took a seat. A lady with long white hair passed by and stopped. She asked if she could join me. We ended up talking about travelling and I mentioned I was going to Scotland.

Well that was it, she told me all about the locations to visit and islands that I had not heard of. In the end I wrote it all down. She was so passionate about the place. She was local to Dartmoor, loved to travel and told me the best places to visit while I was staying on the moor. What a lovely interaction. Anyway we ended up walking back to my van together. She patted Blossom and said 'She is your adventure chariot.' She then made her way over to her van, showed me her fixed bed layout and said 'There is nothing like adVANture.' The word stuck with me. I loved it. We glanced at our watches and realised it was time for food. We both made salads, pulled out our camping chairs and continued to chat.

Finally I had to ask her. 'From everything you have said and how much travel you have done, I literally cannot guess your age.'

She grinned. 'Eighty-two.'

I choked on my food. At eighty-two she was taking adVANtures and did not seem much older than late fifties. 'Travel ignites my soul and keeps me young. The desire to experience has stopped me wanting to depart the world. It is never too late to enjoy life and experience all the world has to offer – even if it is on your doorstep.'

I looked curiously at her. She pointed towards a village in the valley. 'That white cottage on the hill. That is where I live.'

What an inspiration!

CHAPTER 24

WILD SLEEPING

That night I returned to my sleeping destination. I hadn't taken anything out of the van and had already set up the bed. I hadn't put any thermal covers or curtains up and parked with the quickest exit route. I kept my keys where I could reach them and placed my muscle heating spray within grabbing distance. I will be honest, wild camping is fine when there are two of you; however, when there is only one then the mind can play tricks. That means one always needs an escape plan. Mine was simple – the van was prepared for exit and my keys were close by. It may seem extreme but you never know when wild camping, and there is always survival at the back of my mind. It did not help that my dad, who was ex-army always said 'Code word survival'. At ten that night I climbed into my sleeping bag and left the zip unfastened for a quick escape.

By midnight I was asleep, after lots of mental churn and feeling on edge. The moon rose and I could see it through the window. It was a new crescent moon. I saw a few bats fly above. I then drifted off to sleep. At around three in the morning I heard a noise outside and leapt up. I peered out of the window and a badger emerged from the thicket. I watched it plod along and walk into a bush along the way. I settled down again only to be woken by a branch tapping the van. I glanced out and saw two foxes rummaging around outside. First light was emerging and I was feeling a bit shattered. I rolled over and fell asleep until five-thirty. I couldn't sleep, so decided on a couple of coffees and dark chocolate. I then did a meditation CD and felt a bit recharged. The thing was it wasn't enough. I was going to be shattered for most of the day. That is why I generally prefer campsites.

I drove back over to Haytor Rocks and went for an amble. I found a lovely rock, sat on it and took in the view. I had another coffee and was wired. To offset that I drank loads of water, which meant I needed the loo. Since there were no toilets in sight I had to do an alfresco pee. I found a perfect pee-wee location and sighed. I don't like to pee outside or on location because it makes me feel naughty. It is as if I have broken rules. So I shook the lady lettuce, pulled up my knick-naks and screamed. Two horses were standing beside the hedge. They had silently watched the pee-wee proceedings. When I screamed they flinched but did not bolt. I wondered what they made of the situation.

After that I made my way back to the van and decided to visit Becky Falls.

CHAPTER 25

REVERSING UNDER PRESSURE

The narrow lanes were definitely fearsome when it came to driving Blossom. Talk about being pushed to your driving limits when coming face to face with a local bus appearing from the other direction. Of course it had a huge line of traffic behind it. Well unfortunately I had no traffic behind me which meant I was going to have to reverse. The thing is it wasn't just a little reverse instead it was around seven hundred meters to the nearest passing spot behind me. What made it more difficult was the lane was narrow, bendy and had stone walls on either side.

Being shattered from lack of sleep and filled with caffeine, I would say I wasn't in the best state to attempt such a manoeuvre, although necessity is the mother of reversing intervention. The situation forced me to focus. As much as the bus driver looked peeved and impatient I was not going to rush or damage Blossom. So a rather slow and calculated reverse, forward to realign and reverse again took place. I did not rush, instead I thought if I am in this situation then you lot have to deal with it! Admittedly I felt pressured, a bit stressed and could have cried but I sucked it up and focused. After about fifteen minutes (bear in mind there were numerous corners, people on horses, motor bikes and other random anomaly turning up on my reversing path) I made it to the passing area.

I pulled in and watched the bus, around twenty cars, six motor bikes, two horses and a milk float pass by. I glanced in my rear-view mirror. There were only two cars behind me and those two cars were in convenient passing places about fifty meters apart within the village.

I took a deep breath and made it along the lane without the need for another reverse. I have to say that when I arrived at Becky Falls I was relieved and sat for a moment in Blossom reflecting on what a demanding situation that reverse had been and how proud of myself I had been not to panic.

After paying to enter Becky Falls I followed a steep path down beside the river. The air was fresh, there were oaks, beech trees and numerous birch. The canopy was thick with leaves, and the sound of trickling water washed away the reversing anxiety. I found a secluded spot by the river where a tree had fallen, and sat on the beam. The sun was dappled by the branches and the sound of water was relaxing. I was so relaxed I took off my cardigan, placed it on the ground, sat on that and reclined against the tree. Two hours later I woke up. No one had bothered me, maybe no one had noticed me, but I actually felt relaxed and refreshed. It was quite amazing. I checked around me and heard a group of people chatting in the distance but not much more than that. More than anything I heard blackbirds, jays and a few cuckoos.

I went to get up and my goodness I was stiff because I had slept for two hours with my legs crossed. As I went to stand my legs had pins and needles. I almost face-planted as the blood flowed back into my legs. I have to say I found that amazing.

Well I continued the Becky Falls circuit and found trees with coins bashed into them, numerous fallen trees with lichen landscapes and a whole wealth of waterfalls. The area was stunning. I took a couple more 'take in the view' moments along with plenty of photos. Everywhere one looked there was an inspirational vista demanding photographic attention. I must have spent a couple of hours occupied in admiration of nature, waterfalls and the contortions of ancient trees and their roots.

Time was hoovered up again and I had forgotten to eat. Luckily there was a café on site. As much as I would have loved a cream tea, I was eating far too much sugar. In the end I went for a savoury tea which had salad, a cheese scone and a selection of cheeses with two rather nice chutneys.

While I ate I watched a family with a baby. The baby grinned at me mischievously as she picked up her parents chips, squished them in her fingers and then proceeded to smear them around her face. When the parents were distracted by their son, who appeared to be around five, the baby placed her hands in some baked beans and wiped them across her forehead. When the parents turned back it was as if she had created a food face pack. It was funny listening to the parental theories of the food phenomenon.

I took my time there and wrote up my experiences in my journal. I was in a dilemma regarding my sleeping arrangements. Should I return to the same layby or try somewhere else? I had not slept well, although when a place feels familiar it might enable better sleep. In the end I decided I could not be bothered to scope out another location and decided on the same place.

That evening I was excited about eating in a to a well-to-do restaurant with Michelin stars that happened to be in a hotel close to the Haytor Rocks. I booked a table for one and changed into my 'spa clothes'. I will explain that towards the end of the story. Well, I navigated more narrow lanes and came to the conclusion that I disliked them but became very aware of all of the passing places. What I found fascinating was how deft the locals were at rapid reversing. It was easy for them and they did it like professionals.

I chose my seat carefully in the restaurant because I like to sit against the wall and enjoy looking out at everyone. That evening it seemed the restaurant had attracted a retired crowd. Most of the diners appeared to be at least mid-sixties and above. Many of the couples sat in silence as they ate. I glanced at them then studied the menu. There were some lovely food combinations and I wanted to try them all. The problem was I was not terribly peckish after the cheese scone. In the end I decided that I had to attempt gluttony at least once in my life. So I chose a cheese soufflé for starters, followed by a random risotto which was finalised with a caramel cheesecake.

Luckily the food was not served quickly because the soufflé was so tasty, and served with spinach and onion. Each flavour perfectly considered. The risotto was a saffron risotto. The details of the flavour felt like one was taking taste travel through the exotic unknown. As much as I was full, I had to force myself to endure the cheesecake, which was orgasmic in itself. Yep I was stuffed, but it was worth it. I paid the bill and just as I was about to leave a lady wearing gold shoes and a leopard skin dress came over. She asked if I was okay. I said that I was. She had wondered whether I was lonely because I was alone. I found that sweet. 'I am far from lonely, I am enjoying time away from people and doing. It is wonderful plus I love my own company.'

She smiled sweetly and admitted when she was single she felt very lonely. Her and her new husband wanted to make sure I was okay. They wondered if I needed company, if so they would be in the lounge. She then studied me, 'I am glad you are good at being alone. I am not. I wish someone would have come and asked me if I was okay when I was in a restaurant alone. I only did it a few times because I felt a bit embarrassed.'

What a sweet thing to confess to a stranger. 'I have a bit of a different perspective. I like my own company and enjoy going to places and tasting the food properly. When I am with people I find we often talk and don't savour the food. When you are alone you can take your time, not talk and really luxuriate in flavours.'

She appeared stunned, 'Well that is something I never considered. Thank you. I may try going to a restaurant alone with that approach.'

That night I returned to the layby with a very full stomach. I laid down, crashed out and did not wake up until six-thirty in the morning. I slept through and was not disturbed. Feeling refreshed I went for a walk over to Wisteria Woods and indulged in the morning chorus. I sat with my coffee and dark chocolate and prepared for my next stop – Cornwall.

CHAPTER 26

CARVING CORNISH

When I was in my early twenties I used to spend my weekends in Cornwall surfing. There is a certain feeling about the place – it is raw, real and has decent waves. I have always loved it down there, so it made sense to visit some of my old stomping grounds. With that in mind, I stayed at Gwithian, a huge beach close to Hale with a seal sanctuary nearby. The surrounding area had some lovely little cafes. The site I stayed at was close to the dunes and one could stroll down to the sea amongst the wiry grass or across to nearby chalets. The view of the lighthouse was epic when the skies turned red at sunset. The thing was there was yet another storm on its way. Once I was set up and turned into the wind, I accepted that it was probably wise either to stay in the van or go to a café. I decided that the van was the best option because I would have to walk through a wall of blustering sand back to Blossom and that would hurt.

So at five in the evening, I sat in my captain's seat and gazed out of the window. I stared out to sea as a wall of storm rampaged in our direction. At first there were a few windy blasts but it soon became apparent the magnitude of the storm because Blossom shook. I am glad I turned my van in the direction of the wind because the shake wasn't as bad. The larger vans, who hadn't turned, were being battered.

The wind lifted the sand and pelted us. I wondered whether I would wake up to an entirely different paintwork. That evening I made my dinner, listened to an audio book and went to bed early. The storm raged through the night and the whole of the next day. In the end I ventured out wearing sunglasses, even though it wasn't sunny. When I walked towards the café the sand snaked in ghost-like lines through the dunes. The waves were huge and the sky was a murky grey. At one point a flock of seagulls appeared to be flying backwards when a gust of wind caught them.

As I walked I leant into the wind. It was like pushing against an invisible wall. After a while I was puffed out with all of the effort. It really was something! In the end I made it to the café and... it was closed. Not surprising really, why would anyone venture out in that? I continued my strolling circuit and came to the conclusion that I was going to hang out in Blossom until it stopped. I could drive to one of the nearby towns but thought I would take the opportunity to rest and not do much. Instead I would dream, listen to audio books, relax, sketch and catch up with my journal... One has to take 'empty time' opportunity when it presents itself.

While I was in Gwithian I took a stroll to Hale. I walked through the dunes on the way there and on the way back along the beach. My primary goal was to get some shopping without using Blossom as transport. Ironically, after a few detours I managed to walk twelve miles. I have to admit that evening and the following day I did not want to do much. In the end I headed down to the beach and took in the rock pools. Sitting and gazing into rock pools clad with limpets, containing colourful star fish and random seaweeds was deeply relaxing. I actually spent most of the day paddling about and just looking. What forced the rock pool rally to come to a close was the fact the tide came in. I could have spent the rest of the evening there too.

On the way back to Blossom I stopped at a small café on the corner. It was a hidden gem. I ordered a sausage and egg sandwich. I will be honest, I had no idea why I fancied that, I was probably a bit fed up of a diet of fish and veg. Well I sat, and chatted to numerous dog owners and locals. They advised me that there was a nice walk towards the lighthouse with the seal sanctuary nearby. That would be the place to visit the following day.

That evening I had a fruit cider while sitting in the grassy dunes. I watched a spectacular sunset and admired the lighthouse. I could feel that I was warm inside and a sense of contentedness permeated my being. I was so glad that I had taken the trip.

CHAPTER 27

LEISURELY STROLLS

It is funny how one bottle of cider resulted in me waking up at ten in the morning, even though I was in bed by ten that evening. I clearly required a big sleep. The problem is that such a late wake up throws me off. I like my routine and breakfast at eleven just does not do it for me because I missed my coffee and chocolate. Talk about a creature of habit. Well, I decided that time loss dictated that I was not going to cook. I filled my thermos and headed along the beach to another café, which seemed to be a halfway point between the lighthouse and the campsite. Ohhh now they had some lovely food choices. I won't go into details but I chose a rather delicious wrap containing halloumi. The café itself was beside a National Trust carpark, which meant there were plenty of patrons visiting.

I found a bench, ate my wrap and ended up meeting some lovely pups. They obviously scoped me out because I was eating; however, what they did do was enable me to chat to some locals who told me a bit more about the seal sanctuary. They advised me to take a stroll along the beaches before the hill because there were some beautiful rock formations. In addition I discovered some of the cliff had fallen away and that I should stick to the path. That really triggered my fear of edges.

Well thank goodness I met that lovely group because I walked along the beach and spent a lot of time photographing, rocks, scenery and more rock pools. I then took a gradual meander over to the seal sanctuary. There was an alcove of what appeared to be large writhing rocks. There was also a rancid fish aroma in the air. I watched the creatures for a while making their way in and out of the ocean. From a distance they looked like writhing giant slugs. I then glanced at my phone it was already close to five in the evening. Time had ambushed me once more. By the time I got back it would be around six-thirty and that meant I would prepare dinner, head out to the sand dunes for sunset and then bed. The following day was my last full day. Five days had flown – it wasn't enough!

CHAPTER 28

SOMETHING FISHY

My last day was spent visiting St Ives. I headed over there early because it was quite a popular tourist destination. I wanted to make sure I could park without issue. When I followed the Satnav I found a parking spot beside the sports centre on a hill. One could get a bus into town. Why do that when one could explore? I soon realised why the bus was a good option: there were lots of steps and hills to navigate to get to the centre.

When I was in my twenties I used to spend a lot of time in St Ives and had wonderful memories of surfing, art galleries and creativity. I had attended parties on beaches and raves in the caves. It was phenomenal. I used to love it there. Of course the place filled with tourists but it didn't matter because they purchased art.

The first thing I noticed when I walked the back streets to the Tate gallery was how things had changed. All of the little arty nooks and crannies had been bought up by 'outsiders' during the Covid plague. People could work from home, which meant many people purchased a second home or moved out of cities. Where St Ives had once been an art community it seemed that the artist had either become incredibly wealthy or moved on. My gut instinct erred towards 'moved on' because where there had once been sculptures and art on forecourts there were now Tesla, Ferrari, Bugatti, Audis and Porsche. That particular day the wealthy owners had taken to polishing their pride and joys on their forecourts or drives. The arty area had completely transformed. I wondered whether the Tate was still in pride of place. Had that been purchased by an 'out of towner?'

I rounded a corner and breathed a sigh of relief because that wonderful architecture stood pride of place overlooking the bay. What's more, I was lucky enough to be there when there was an exhibition of botanical art. Since I loved forests, nature and ecosystems I spent a couple of hours absorbing the art into my cells and came out enlivened at around midday.

After saturating myself with the artistic delights, I made my way to one of my favourite cafes/restaurants overlooking a bay. I took a seat at an area gazing out onto the beach and watched surfers jostling for peak position on waves. My memories flooded back and I simply sat smiling until a waft of an aroma that resembled doom graced my nostrils. The smile was wiped from my face as another waft prickled a nostril.

A moment later a waiter came to take my order. I asked whether something evil had happened on the floor below because there was a hideous hum in the air. He sniffed and gagged. 'I think you should move,' he said.

I relocated to a corner booth that was up wind and placed my order. I also mentioned the fact that the back streets had changed from arty to extremely wealthy. He told me that things had really changed and many of the cottages had become second homes, or people had moved there from cities. That had affected the house prices and made hospitality a nightmare. The local food and hotel businesses could not get staff because of Brexit and the cost for a young person to live in the town was beyond what they could earn. The result was no staff and a number of the cafes had to close.

It was such a shame. He took my order and returned with a grin. 'I found the stink,' he said triumphantly.

The chef is making a fish sauce for the curry evening. Apparently it smells rancid but tastes amazing. I frowned, as much as he was selling it to me, the thought of tasting something that smelled like rotten intestine did not appeal.

My food arrived and it was as delicious as I remembered. I loved that café and view. I took my time and tipped him. He needed as much help as possible to be able to live there. Of course the conversation about people moving from cities to a beautiful village which priced the locals out of the market bothered me. St Ives had always had a community atmosphere. It also had a vibrant surf and art culture. When I was younger a lot of young people rebelled against careers, settled in the area and gave art or music a go. Many did well, some failed and others took different life directions. That same opportunity would be diminished if the cost of living exceeded the wages. There would ultimately be a long-term effect. At that time it was just the tip of the iceberg.

A nice meander around the town where I popped into some art galleries and purchased some locally printed T-shirts was just what I needed. It was lovely to potter, to see what was popular for tourists to buy. It seemed local brews, ales, ciders, gins, pickles and fudge were at the top of the list. It made sense, it was all stuff you could take home and share.

On my return I strolled past the quay area and watched the tourist throngs. I then glanced through a gap between buildings and saw the most enormous mobile home attempting to manoeuvre. Whoever it was had taken a wrong turn into narrow lanes. Now they had to navigate through the warren with an abundance of tourists walking on the road. I was glad I had parked on the outskirts, even if it did mean scaling numerous steps and steep hills.

On my way home I was reflective. My memories of being young, surfing and partying in the arty town played through my mind. It is at times like that you realise that you lived in a wonderful era and had definitely made the most of everything without knowing how things would change. Wasn't that life though? One always has to make the best of what is now because in the future you look back and say those were the good times. I feel as though the lesson there was about community and division. Why did wealth create division? Maybe over time the whole town would become a wealth magnet, which would become its own community.

My last evening was spent sitting on a bench watching the sunset and being reflective. The air was warm, the clouds were gold, red and orange. The light made the grass shimmer and rabbits darted amongst the gorse. That night was a pivotal point in the journey because I was about to change direction and drive to Glastonbury.

CHAPTER 29

GLASTONBURY - LEARNING TO JUST STOP

I have noticed that when I visit places I feel that I should literally arrive and get out there and explore. I like to get my bearings and see what the place is like. It is all so exciting out there - with so many options. The problem is I forget to chill out and just be. I have realised my planning tendency means that I have an itinerary which stops me from just going with the flow and let things unfold. With that in mind, I took a slow drive to Glastonbury and arrived in the evening because I had arranged for an allocated spot. When I arrived I marvelled at the lovely and well organised campsite right beside the Tor. It had a shop, electrical hook-up and had themed food evenings. Lovely!

Once I was shown my pitch, I spent my time pottering around and set up my bed. Blossom was all cosy and I gazed up at the ceiling to be greeted by a rather leggy spider-beauty who had snuck in for the evening. Since I had no 'weapons' - like a cordless vacuum cleaner, I had to use my back-up pee-wee cup and my dark chocolate cardboard cover to capture the beast and launch it out of the door unharmed.

The thing is you get all 'itchy-bottomed' after such incidents and even your sleeping bag touching your skin can make you nervy... So after that little spidery essay, I always have a huge plastic cup and piece of cardboard ready. I then prepare for the pursuit with van door open for plastic cup propulsion. For those that don't believe in karma, take a pre-charged vacuum cleaner with you. Personally I don't like to kill creepy-crawlies and prefer throwing random unused peewee cups from the van accompanied by inane screaming to ingratiate myself with fellow campers. Of course I make sure I breathily repeat the word 'SPIDER' loud enough to justify my random hurling of vacuous items.

After the spider incident I had to go for a stroll to remove myself from the spider scene and to enable any adrenalin to be processed before bed. The amble was also an opportunity to get my campsite bearings. Even that little wander reiterated that Glastonbury certainly had an energy and history. Just beyond the campsite I discovered two very ancient trees, Gog and Magog. When I say ancient trees, they were mighty, vast and you could sense their age by the size of their trunks. To provide an idea of the size, one of the trunks was at least eleven foot in diameter and had over two thousand rings.

The green 'Glastonbury giants' were absolutely fascinating and I only noticed them when a couple were stood beside them taking photos. I waited for the couple to depart and then went and read the plinth beside them. The two trees were called Gog and Magog after the biblical giants. There is a lot of mythology behind them which ties in with Avalon, the Tor and Paganism. The pair are known as the oaks of Avalon and stand at the entrance point of Avalon. Unfortunately the tree named Gog is dead and Magog was close to stepping into the other world. Talking of other worlds –

it was nearing bedtime and I needed to make sure I was spider-free.

CHAPTER 30

RAINBOW KNITWEAR REBELLION

What I love about Glastonbury is that there are quite often peaceful demonstrations taking place. On this particular occasion there was a demonstration against capitalism. This demonstration was actually rather lovely. At first I misinterpreted it for a musical procession because a huge group of people with drums, singing bowls, tuning forks and shakers marched up to the Tor playing their instruments. It was only when I saw some banners that said 'Capitalist Greed needs to end'. 'Say no to Capitalism' and 'Greed is NOT good,' that the capitalist rebellion penny dropped.

I have to say that procession was probably the most colourful demonstration I have ever seen. The knitwear was splendid because there were all manner of colourful jumpers, some with rainbows and others with vibrant patterns. That teamed with multi-coloured dreadlocks woven with different silks and wools. Even though it was anti-capitalism the whole procession was like a party. Music, chanting and dancing. I ended up chatting to one of the participants who advised me at mid-day the group would peacefully chant together around the Tor. How lovely! She said that I was welcome to join. I glanced at the sky, as much as it might have been an experience, the foreboding weather doom put me off. Plus I would have been a bit of a hypocrite because I wasn't against capitalism as such, I was for a better option. Unfortunately a better option has not been presented or suggested, so there is nothing to move towards or transition into. Until I can witness a better option then the system we reside in will suffice because it enables survival.

With all of that in mind, I continued along the path and paused to watch the procession wind up to the Tor. I am glad I witnessed such a peaceful gathering. I was quite touched by the approach. I took a different path up to the other side of the Tor and glanced up at the sky. A thwack of thunder and flare of lightning initiated a huge rumbling which resulted in a thunderous torrent. All those lovely people sitting chanting against capitalism were soaked. I felt for them. I wondered how long they would chant for during such conditions.

As the rain poured, my 'just in case' polka dot poncho became a saviour. As ridiculous as I looked, and how it certainly did not match anything, that fold down poncho protected me from what felt like an emergence of a waterfall from the heavens. I know this might sound weird for some - but there is a strange smug satisfaction that can be felt when wearing a polka dot poncho and flapping your arms as you make your way along a path. No one knew me and the polka dots seemed to trigger my need to be random in and around Glastonbury. No eye-lids were batted because a lot of them were closed due to chanting focus and the area is very accepting of weirdness. Being 'normal' was the new weird.

After strolling up the Tor and peering down across the countryside in the rain, I decided to make my way into Glastonbury. It was a bit of a 'get my bearings' opportunity and since it was still relatively early, I felt there was prime opportunity to go with the flow. Especially because I was in Glastonbury which was famous for the wells.

Well what I love is when you make random discoveries. On this occasion I discovered a 'peace garden' it was on the road from the Tor leading into Glastonbury town centre. I arrived just as it opened and had the place to myself. The garden was wonderful, beautiful flowers, old contorted trees and water arrangements that flowed through and around the grounds. There were benches dotted here and there to sit and just take it all in. The atmosphere there was truly tranquil. Of course something had to disrupt the quiet. On the other side of the garden wall a chap was giving a couple a piece of his mind about how capitalism just meant greed and that everyone should be able to live freely. No one should have to work and we should all be given enough money to do what we want. What a lovely concept. I won't go into my mental response. The couple he was talking to seemed a little resistant to his great idea. 'If no one worked then who would pay the tax to give you the money to do nothing?' One asked.

There was a drawn silence.

'If no one worked then how would food be produced and transported?' Said the other part of the couple.

Another silence.

'What about houses? How would houses be built if no one built them?' One of the couple asked.

I was excited to hear his solution.

'I knew it! Your clothes give you away! I see you are capitalists... See there is always someone that supports the stupid ideas of the rich. That is the problem. 'THEY' are controlling your mind. You need to be free. Anyway I have to get back because I have an Amazon delivery,' he said and scurried away.

The couple were silent. I could imagine they simply glanced at each other with knowing looks.

I wondered whether the conversation was the universe being comical in answer to my question – is there a better way. Well, I took my time in the peace garden and then popped out onto the street where a woman in her fifties wearing a navy striped apron was selling coffee and cake from her van. I purchased a piece of coffee and walnut cake with a coffee and returned to the garden. A little voice whispered, 'Capitalism will remain until there is something better to move to. Unless there is something to move towards then change will not come.'

I looked around to check whether anyone else had heard my mental whispering. There was no one around, the atmosphere was completely silent, which is of course when inspiration came. I ended up spending another couple of hours in the garden. I couldn't bring myself to leave. Often I feel sad when a wonderful experience comes to an end, so attempt to indulge in it as much as possible.

While in Glastonbury I felt the urge to either have a reading or some healing. As it turned out I managed to time my entrance into a tarot reader's shop when she had two hours between bookings. Well I thought I would create the perfect Glastonbury disguise/blend in by wearing white and purple batik leggings, a pink leopard skin top, knee-high outdoor boots and a multi-coloured scarf. To top it off I wore the wonderfully flappy polka dot poncho. The absolute lack of coordination, randomness and just lack of colour consideration made me a chameleon, or so I thought. That is a stark contrast to my smartish attire, which is usually a maximum of two considered colours in a classic style. Even though I had gone to town in my inability to combine colours and patterns, apparently I had tourist written all over me. Bum!

The psychic smiled an enigmatic smile and went to town on her reading. She was pretty spot on and my poker face cracked a few times. She told me that I had a chariot that I was making a big adventure in. The journey ahead would provide deep insights into myself, life and what was possible. I would transform during the journey and return to my original normality a whole new person. She also thought that I would move house and find my true love by the end of the year. She said when I returned to work I would have great success and a pay rise.

That all sounded very positive. So I handed over the cash and stepped outside. A downpour ensued which was the perfect opportunity to adorn my polka dot poncho once more and flap about smugly. The procession of protestors about climate change marched back through the centre of Glastonbury chanting and singing in their lovely rainbow coloured knitwear and... the rain became torrential. The group continued to chant and wave their butterfly and bee flags. No one grumbled or seem peeved. Instead they sung, danced and demonstrated. How wonderful!

Along the road, a busker with no talent at all started singing 'It's Raining Men' out of tune. It was certainly quite random, but strangely comforting. I continued up the high street to a health food shop. Ohhh and I was sooooo happy because they had raw dark chocolate. They had my favourite one too with nuts and peanut butter. Could the day get any better?

While I salivated at the shelf, a couple considered the raw chocolate options and I recommended my favourite. They took my advice and told me they were there for the week from 'up North'. They had heard of Glastonbury and the fact that it was rather alternative but had been surprised by the amount of crystals, chanting and psychics all found in one area. They had visited the Tor and were stunned by the undulation of the surrounding hills. It was astounding what one finds out when recommending dark chocolate. The couple were having a lovely time and were really pleased to visit a place that made them feel so relaxed. I asked them whether they had noticed the 'shit busker'. They hadn't but they were intrigued to discover how bad that busker really was. When I passed by the busker he was singing that he was sexy and he knew it. He definitely wasn't sexy and might have been deluded. He should have sung I'm sexy and deluded instead. Well, it all added to the experience.

In the end I stayed a couple more days and wafted around Glastonbury, went for nice walks near the campsite and allowed myself just to sit and read in my fold-out chair. I wanted to take it easy and enjoy. I have to say I saw a lot of bats, some rats, a couple of mice, voles and plenty of buzzards out on the walks. The evenings were warm with golden light cast over the fields and the silhouette of the Tor stood overlooking the surrounding hills. There was something magical about being there. I loved it!

CHAPTER 31

BIRTHDAY DUNKING

So, my adVANture had to factor in a friend's birthday, she was based in Wimborne. Prior to the adVANture we had said we would get three of us together to paddle board. Mandy is my ex-rowing partner. She and I used to compete all over the country a few years ago; however, a random set of events involving another rowing club and me and my big mouth ended up with Mandy meeting the love of her life. Basically I spotted the chap, thought he would suit Mandy and that was it. I 'TOLD' them they were meant for each other and they were. Three years later they were married. Four years later they had their first child and six years later their second. It all worked out well, other than Mandy and I couldn't compete at rowing anymore.

On my fortieth birthday she introduced me to paddle boarding, when our rowing was winding down. I have to say that was fortuitous because it meant that I did not have to compete or train for so many hours to remain at peak fitness. I will be honest, I came to the end of my need to compete in my early forties, so endless training to win felt pointless. What's more, my coach found out my actual age. Until then he had assumed I was in my early thirties (rather than early forties). It might have been something to do with the fact that I was not terribly mature because I was very sociable and always out and about. I had a lot of energy, worked hard and always enjoyed a good gathering. The coach told me I couldn't compete with or against the youngens and had to join the veteran team. That was the end of it and paddle boarding became my water indulgence.

So with that in mind, it was Mandy's birthday and her husband had agreed to look after the kiddiwinks as a bit of a pressie. The truth was she had not taken a day away from the kiddies since her daughter was born. Mandy and I decided to have a day paddle boarding and have a nice lunch at Aunt Fannies near Wimborne. So... I tailored my big trip to travel along the South coast, around Cornwall, up to Glastonbury and back home for the paddle board fun and would then set off the following day for Scotland via the Cotswolds and the lakes.

In a strange way the route worked out well because I popped home, did my washing, checked that everything was okay and had a lovely time with my buddies. Half of me considered camping in Blossom on my parking space so that I could honestly say that I lived in my van the whole time. The thing was sometimes one needs their own bed.

Mandy and I had a mutual friend, Karen who also paddle boarded, so it seemed a lovely idea for us all to spend the day on the river. There was nothing like having a picnic on a paddle board amongst beautiful nature-filled surroundings. Admittedly, I treated the day with my pals in the same way as I approached the rest of the adVANture – I lived the moment, I didn't 'do' any computers and made the best of the short time visiting a place.

That morning we all met up by a bridge on the River Stour. Both of my buddies had not been as 'exercise aware' as they used to be and both mentioned that straight away. Funnily enough I had arrived early and noticed the river was high and fast flowing. I was fine with that because I always go up stream and if the current is strong it washes you back down. It is like cycling up hill. I do the same on the sea with the wind. I paddle into the wind and then use it to blow me home, as long as the wind direction does not change then you can feel a little bit smug as you glide back home. If it does change then you have to paddle like buggery to get back to land. Not that I know how anyone paddles like buggery. Strange image really. Probably best not to think about it.

After we all greeted each other with a group-cuddle, we inflated our paddle boards and I gave Mandy her pressie. I had purchased a gin liqueur with rhubarb and ginger in the camping shop in Glastonbury. It was lovely to say the least and definitely warmed your cockles up, of course we had to have a taste before launching.

When it came to launching I had my wetsuit socks, Karen had her wetsuit booties and Mandy wore flip flops. At that moment I clocked something didn't feel right and my gut flipped. Of course we continued anyway. The sun was out, there was blue sky and a river to paddle.

From the offset the paddle was testing. I was fine but realised my friends were challenged and did not want to admit it. I slowed down when we came to a fast flowing section and stopped paddling. I found myself gliding backwards at speed. That was another alarm bell in my mind. The speed I was going backwards at was faster than I had experienced in a while. Down the river there was a weir too. What made the situation increasingly concerning was there were no other paddle boarders or kayaks. Admittedly we launched at a remote place and it was mid-week which made the lack of other paddler's scenario most likely.

When my friends reached the gushing area, we climbed off the boards and walked through the shallows to a calmer area. The thing was you could feel the power of the current beneath the surface. That again made me feel queasy. Of course we all joked about the hidden power and force of water. One never knew what was going on beneath the surface.

We continued paddling for an hour and finally Karen said she needed to stop because she was getting tired. Just as she said that she was caught on the current and collided with Mandy. I was up stream and turned around and laughed. Unfortunately it was no laughing matter because Mandy fell in and was swept underwater by the current to a deeper area. She emerged downstream gasping for breath. Now, Mandy and I used to compete at rowing in the most ridiculous conditions and we both know to stay calm. She remained composed but the current had her. Karen and

I turned around and paddled after her, caught up and directed her to the shallows where she coughed up water. As much as she was a strong woman, she had been under too long and had run out of breath. Karen couldn't apologise enough because she had accidentally knocked her off her board.

'Imagine dying on your birthday,' Mandy said trying to make a joke of it. Unfortunately the reality hit that she would have left a young family behind.

I asked what Mandy wanted to do and she said she wanted to continue up river – 'to get back on the horse' where we would stop and have a mini-snack picnic. I asked if she was sure and she was definite about it. She said nearly drowning should not affect a person's pleasure. I was dubious; however, it was her decision on her birthday. So we continued up stream to a lovely little bay area with swans nearby. On the far banks we watched kingfisher and heron going about their daily lives. The reeds were fresh and there were willows on the other side of the river. We basked in the sun for a while and caught up with all of our news. It was lovely. Admittedly, I could see Mandy was shaken and attempting to maintain a brave face. Karen seemed edgy because she had knocked our friend off her board, even by accident, and felt responsible for Mandy's near-death experience.

Anyway, after snacks, the best part of paddling up a river was gliding back. We all climbed on our boards and the sensation of gliding and flowing down river on our boards in unison was beautiful. The speed at which we travelled with the river was immense. There was no effort - just ease. What it made you realise was how much effort you had put in to paddle against the current. We had really given it some welly! Essentially we went through the struggle first to be rewarded with the feeling of flow with ease on the return. Absolute bliss!

After such an adventure it was customary to go to lunch and over-eat because you 'definitely deserved it'. Funnily enough, when we arrived Mandy said she felt a fatty but was going to enjoy a proper birthday lunch. We went to Aunt Fannies and found a table with benches each side. Mandy sat down and the bench snapped in half. She fell backwards with her legs in the air. It happened right in the middle of the restaurant too. On top of that she really bashed her head. Once more she made the situation into an amusing spectacle and patted her stomach. 'Too much birthday cake.'

I was concerned for her. Something seemed to be going on with her. Rather than enjoying herself, everything seemed to be turning into a bit of a disaster.

Finally, when we questioned her, she broke into tears. She was exhausted, which made her clumsy, lose coordination and made her accident-prone. She said she was so looking forward to having a girl's day, and that she didn't want to ruin it. I gave her a cuddle and held space for her. She sobbed, 'The worst thing is I feel guilty for having some time away from my babies.'

It occurred to me that my lovely friend was struggling but kept going even though she needed a break.

She sighed and said 'I wish I still had my freedom and I am so jealous - in a nice way of your adVANture… Please do me a favour… Write it up and share it with me so that I can imagine what it is like and go on the journey with you.'

Hmmmm. I will be honest… I was only going to journal this stuff for me, for when I am old but as I am the reliable sort I decided to honour my birthday buddy and write up the adVANtures. I will gift it to her on her next birthday – if I can complete it in that time. Who knows? I have to admit, that set of events reminded me that you never know when your number is up. There has been a common theme on the journey – make the most of your now. Who knows what is around the corner? I also realised you have to make the most of everything and your friends will love you even when you are struggling. They are there for you. With that in mind, when I went home, I luxuriated in the comfort of my bed. Enjoyed the smell of my fresh washing and re-packed my van according to what I had not used. Strangely the forced return and my reliability had served me well, although not so much for my friends. I had recharged and refocused by having one day at home. That meant I had clarity and knew how to approach phase two of the trip.

CHAPTER 32

BEAUTIFUL BIBURY

Quite often when you are making a big trip people give you advice on places to visit. Sometimes these places are great and other times they don't really do anything for you. On this occasion my brother had mentioned that on my way to the Cotswolds it was definitely worth stopping off at Bibury. All I can say is wow! Bibury is a small village in the Cotswolds, which is known for its beauty. I found a nice little carpark on the edge of the village by a trout farm, and took a saunter along the river. There were stone bridges and an atmosphere filled with history. Such villages have a cream tea ambience along with coffee and cake necessity. I do like cake.

What I also find with such flower-filled villages is that one's body relaxes just by being there. It wasn't as if I was stressed; however, I felt my shoulders visibly drop when I saw the line of historic houses which are regularly depicted in the 'beautiful village pictures' found on the net. Well, I had a few hours until I could check in at my campsite which was just thirty minutes away, so thought I would circumnavigate the village using the footpaths.

As I strolled, a swan with five fluffy cygnets elegantly glided along the river. The water was clear with plenty of pondweed undulating in the current. The sun came out and the blue sky reflected in the water. A bench caught my attention and I felt it was time to just take in the beauty. Since it was still very early in the morning there weren't many people around and the little village didn't have a rush hour. Something I have noticed when travelling is that it is very easy to 'route march' around a place rather than be present and enjoy. That is probably down to our 'doing culture' where we have to 'do, produce, deliver and experience'. Could you imagine going to a beautiful place and not taking a picture now? I sat for a while just watching the swans and the grey fluff-balls darting about on the surface of the water. It was pleasant to just be, and not have to log in, work or produce. I could enjoy watching nature and little fluff-balls experiencing their physicality on a river. It was bliss.

After a while I took a stroll along the famous avenue filled with the charming historic houses. I love the rose displays and the pride that the villagers took in their homes. I am always fascinated by gardens, trellises, and the time people spend selecting garden flowers to cultivate and nurture. Once more I took my time, admired the combination of fragrances and floral beauty, and felt the atmosphere. I ended up chatting to some locals who were walking their dogs and they took a picture of me with the houses in the background. They told me that I was visiting at the ideal time, before the tourist influx. They said by eleven in the morning the place would be crawling with holidaymakers. I took that into consideration – I had two and a half hours until the mass tourist crawling began.

I followed a path up the hill, found myself a rather lovely walk through trees, across the back of the village and back down through some fields. Nothing exciting happened, instead it was just nice to absorb the peace, sit on a wall and be in a state of stillness. There was no rush, instead there was a meadow vistas, daisies, dandelions and spatterings of poppies. I took numerous deep breaths and filled my lungs. I have to admit that breath work took me into a heightened state. Lovely!

My meander back to the village enabled me to meet some more dog walkers who lived locally. They suggested that I go to the trout farm where there was a nice café. There I could indulge in proper coffee and cake. I took their advice (there was clearly no resistance) and selected a well-iced piece of lemon sponge. I took a seat overlooking the trout farm. It was so simple and there was no rush other than the sugar rush from eating cake. I sat just watching, admiring and contemplating. I realised there didn't need to be any real events when visiting a place, one could simply waft about and go with the flow. It was enough. During my world travels I often desired to find stories or to return to the ship and tell tales of random events. In this situation I was content: a beautiful village, fluff-ball cygnets experiencing life and a delicious piece of cake. It was simple and a delight. Taking time to smell the roses was something I intended to do more often. I realised that joy can simply creep into your heart and fill you. There is no action, instead she is like a phantom that ignites your heart when you least expect it. The expansion came to a close when I glanced over my shoulder and noticed an influx of cars. The 'crawling tourists' were arriving. It was time to find my campsite and see what wonders were waiting for me there.

CHAPTER 33

CALM, COOL AND CAMPING

One of the things that really appeals to me about having Blossom is that when you lie in the van you can gaze out at some of the most phenomenal views from your rock n' roll bed. In the case of the Cotswolds, I positioned my van beside the lake. The rear view window provided a spectacular vision of the fluffy white clouded dotted sky reflected on pristinely still water. The reflection was crisp and clear. Not a ripple in sight. To the right of me, my two large side windows pointed to a view of a caravan, willows and a long lawn. Obviously I could have positioned my van so the side windows glanced over the lake; however, I found it comfortable to just lay on my stomach glancing out of the rear window. I could see enough of the lake and was not to be bothered by the caravan, which was about twenty meters away. The only thing about that caravan was the almighty posterioral explosion that took place on the first night. It scared the heck out of me and made me scream. Unfortunately the combination of the sound of a rupturing sphincter and a scream was enough to wake up most of the site… Woops. I will elaborate shortly. Of course you are in sphincter suspense now.

Now, the reason I write about the view is that I never take it for granted. I have stayed in some lovely hotels, which cost a lot per night, yet laying on your rock n' roll bed gazing out at the lake was an even better bliss.

To make matters increasingly luxurious Blossom has a rotatable captain's seat, so I can sit reading and glance out of the window with my legs resting on the bed. It really is a pleasure, whether it is raining or sunny. What's more, some of the sunrises and sunsets from the van have been absolutely awe inspiring. The more I reflect on it, the more I realise what a joy it is to be able to witness such phenomenon. Of course there are times when it is minus two outside, you are wrapped up in your sleeping bag and the heat has drained out of the windows. There is condensation and you think 'Blooming 'eck it's nippy!' You wonder whether an icicle may well actually form on any exposed appendages, but that is all part of the adVANture. Over time you discover the right kit and the right way. Admittedly visiting the porta potty isn't terribly appealing when it's cold, but at least you can go to the loo with a view too. Yep that rhymes nicely. The only thing is it can be a bit chilly, plus the whole sleeping bag wrestle to go to the loo does strengthen the bladder because one resists getting up and attempts to stay in the warmth of the down for as long as possible.

At the other end of the scale: summer nights, when the weather is warmer departing the sleeping bag in the night is more appealing. First light generally unfolds pre-five in the morning so one can see what one is doing. Talking of first light, as lovely as it is to watch sunrise, sometimes it is more appealing to sleep. That is why I have blackout curtains. You can swipe them open quickly rather than remove all of the suckers from thermal light blocking screens. Anyway these are all techniques I have developed to enjoy van life. Everyone finds their own ways and as mentioned before, there is something so wonderful about lying in a van gazing out at spectacular scenery and not having to be anywhere or do anything... Bliss!

That evening I cooked my dinner on my outside grill, gazing out over the lake. My neighbours were not around, so I indulged in a nice relaxing evening lounging in one of my fold-out seats. My fairy lights decorated Blossom and I watched ducks bobbing around on the water. I saw two water voles too because I was sitting very still and enjoying. Across in the reeds there were egrets and a heron. How adorable! A state of peace filled me once more and I went to bed when the stars became clear and the moon had risen. That too reflected in the lake and provided a sense of timeless eternity.

I read the paragraph above and the state of peace was bliss in contrast to being woken by what can only be likened to an urgent walrus mating call. It was so loud and intense that it actually made me jump and scream. What is particularly amazing about that was the storm force winds, torrential rain and geese having a gaggling bonanza at other campsites had not made me stir but then... Thwaaaaarp! 2.11am was when posterial hell broke loose.

The funny thing is I had not heard my neighbours return. I must have been in the depths of sleep. I didn't even notice the car engine or the slamming of doors, car boots or rustling of bags. I must have been out for the count until the 'posterial awakening'. Twaaaaaaaaaaaaaaaaarrrppp!

This morning I gazed at my neighbours through my tinted glass. She is a portly, robust-looking woman and he is a slender dejected-looking man. He looked deflated - literally. So my money is on him. He has 'phantom' written all over him. The thing is I am unable to converse with them now because all I can see in my mind is a walrus rearing up and making an urgent mating call. It was terrifying. In my half-asleep state I thought a storm had blown in, ripped through Blossom and taken on a whole new twist.

Luckily my neighbours departed early that morning after taking their dog for walkies. Luckily there were no embarrassing conversations referencing noises in the night. I did wonder whether the phantom had heard the scream, or whether any of the other vaneers had been woken by the catastrophic bottomy cry followed by a scream. It wasn't as if I was going to ask.

You know what? The site was so lovely that I decided to mooch around, chill out and be quiet for the day. I found different areas around the lake and just laid on a picnic blanket gazing at the sky. There was nothing epic or eventful – it was just nice. Admittedly in the afternoon I had to put my rubbish in the bin and refill my water. In doing so I ended up chatting to different mobile home owners who all gave me a tour of their set ups. One had a bed that spun round and a shower that had a rotating door. They were beautiful vans with immensely comfortable interiors. It would be something I may aspire to; however, raising the funds for such luxuries would be trickier. The common denominator amongst the luxury mobile home owners was they had retired.

CHAPTER 34

GNOME STALKERS

On my last night I decided to go to the other end of the site because there were a few little footpaths and an area of woodland I hadn't explored. At this point I need to mention before we continue into a fairy and gnome wonderland is the site is an 'adult only' campsite. I didn't purposely book for that reason, however, the following magical experience might make you believe the place was tailored for children.

Who could have thought that one could be stalked by gnomes? It seemed that everywhere I went there was a gnome peeking from a random fairy door or a secret nook or cranny. So much so, I wondered whether word was out in the gnome world what Teresa had said to my boss regarding going to a Gnome Sanctuary for the big trip. 'She's going to a Gnome Sanctuary.' Obviously there are numerous ways to interpret that:

- A sanctuary for gnomes to keep gnomes safe
- A sanctuary for people with gnomes present
- A sanctuary created by gnomes

Needless to say the boss's response of 'She is a bit odd isn't she?' might appeal perfectly apt. I still find the situation rather amusing. I also can imagine the silence amongst the board of directors as they all contemplated that I would put my job on the line to go to a Gnome Sanctuary. Well that little ditty certainly formed an interesting opinion of me, although what then unfolded was uncanny.

On my last night at the campsite I noticed a sign that pointed to a nice patch of woodland by the lake. In my adVANture relaxation state I wafted in a direction where there were willows, birch and a few horses in a nearby field. I followed a little sign which pointed to an area of woodland and opened a gate. I paused and smirked as I went through. A gnome sat on a swing hanging from a tree. I had just entered a magical place called Gnome Hollow. A gnome peeked out from the branches of a tree. Imagine my surprise. Had Teresa known something I didn't? So I went for a little wander around the 'hollow' and found a bird cage filled with flowers, fake butterflies, and some random painted ladybirds. On some of the trees there were some rather fun bird feeders. I followed the path beside some nesting cottages and a lovely pond filled with lilies. The area felt enchanted especially because the evening light made the trees golden and beams cut through the canopy. They illuminated moss-clad tree stumps with fairies sitting on them. My inner child was ignited.

As I continued I discovered large decorated wooden butterflies nestled on tree trunks, some little fairy doors and houses. There were even some mini-gnomes and fairies perched on logs. I think my favourite area was a series of small houses with lots of fake mushrooms that had been painted various colours. Just beyond those were some little gnome windmill homes and lighthouses. As I continued I came across a sign which said 'Fairy Wood'. Fairies sat beneath decorated toadstools amongst forget-me-not flowers with the aroma of wild garlic. A fluffy black cat decided to join me and meowed as I explored. It was uncanny – I had discovered Gnome Hollow and a fairy village at an adult only campsite. On the way back to Blossom I found the ornately decorated lighthouses on the edge of the pond particularly sweet. It was all so well considered and definitely brought a smile to the face. I think the fact it was all so innocent made it adorable.

I found a carved wooden bench with a sign beside it that said 'Rest a while' and did. The evening light dappled the trees and illuminated everything. Beams broke through the oak canopy and lit up the lilies on the pond. A sense of calm washed through me as I sat quietly amongst the fairies and gnomes. I came to the conclusion to be 'away with the fairies or chilling with the gnomes' really wasn't a bad thing, instead I would recommend it. Silence, peace and serenity does a lot for the soul. I needed to take more of that time.

I sat for a while and noticed the breeze picking up. Some ominous dark clouds spanned the horizon and were moving in our direction. When I say 'our' I mean me, the gnomes and the fairies. I sensed it was time to return to the van and I did so through a meadow with a lovely white pony. I saw a sign which said 'Dingly Dell' beside a lake with a wonderfully elaborate duck mansion. They certainly had a view that evening because the reflection of clouds on the lake was crisp and pristine. Dark clouds, golden light and smatterings of blue sky perfectly reflected... Bliss, calm and serenity resonated through the air. I had accidentally stumbled upon a Gnome Sanctuary and that sanctuary had definitely provided healing. I would let Teresa know she was clearly psychic or had a connection to the invisible gnome world. Although that wasn't the last of the gnomes.

CHAPTER 35

PRIVACY TENT TRIALS

After having such a lovely time it is always sad to pack up and move on. I am generally reluctant about packing up because there are usually a few irksome items to fold or conquer. I often wonder whether anyone else has publically wrestled a privacy tent. When I say wrestle - I haven't actually taken to WWF wrestling (yet) and there are no eye masks, capes or golden lycra; however, public wrestling generally ensues when it comes to awnings and privacy tents.

Like many of the vaneers, I use my privacy tent as storage. In my opinion it is a clever decoy. Who is going to break into a privacy tent to steal a porta potty? If they do then good luck to them because they have to be weird. Picture being caught red handed legging it with a porta loo. Imagine explaining that to a police officer. 'Yes officer I like to run with a porta potty because it builds stamina...' Anyway, I digress... So basically on the last morning of my Cotswold's experience yet another storm became lively and my privacy tent began moving around like a 'curious trouser snake'.

One large gust later, and it was floundering on the ground on its side. As many adVANturers have experienced there is a certain technique to putting away a privacy tent and it can't be rushed. That is where my endeavours went very wrong. Rushing, gustiness and a sail-like entity resulted in a public display of wrestle-mania (like no other). I had the bloomin' thing in a double nelson a few times, and attempted a run up and a body slam. but failed dismally. All the while, the motorhome lovelies watched in dismay from the luxury of their mo-home mansions. The contrast of the privacy tent and the 'tiddler' of a van provided quite a stupendous pre-departure spectacle.

In the end I dragged the blooming thing from public scrutiny and continued my breathy contortions inside the van only to realise it now appeared as though I was having a 'hump-fest' with a privacy tent. There was a lot of rocking without any cocking. I finally admitted defeat and placed the blighter under the bed, which remained fully extended until the torrential rain and gusts ceased. In the meantime, I switched on my phone and went to one of the lady vaneer social media forums and explained my tent wrestling extravaganza. I asked for help and imagine this – one of the fellow lady vaneers made a short film on privacy tent folding and posted it. When the rain stopped I smugly emerged from the van, cast my privacy tent to the ground and folded it like a professional. My neighbours actually opened their window and clapped. I curtseyed and maintained a smug expression as I packed away my last things and prepared for the next phase of the journey.

CHAPTER 36

HAPPY HAT BRIGADE

After rising at sunrise: 4.30ish, watching the geese with their goslings, packing up and wresting the privacy tent, I made the longest journey I have ever done in one go. What's more, it was the furthest north I have driven. What an adVANture. When I arrived I set up, positioned my fold-out chairs and gazed out over Ullswater Lake near Pooley Bridge, in the Lake District. I reflected on the fact I had travelled a four and a half hour blissful drive on the M6 from the Cotswolds. The journey was not what I expected because there was barely any traffic. I have to admit I had been anxious about the journey because I had heard about Spaghetti Junction but somehow ended up taking the toll road. There were a few cars here and there; however, most of the journey was a graceful glide in Blossom with variable weather. What made the trip increasingly enjoyable was that I was lucky enough to travel during the gaps in storms, only a bit of drizzle to contend with and the wind had dropped. As mentioned in the previous writing: the last couple of weeks had been storm after storm, hailstorms, torrential rain and even snow. Surely at the end of May it should be sunny and at least twenty-one degrees... but no... My epic adVANture certainly pushed every weather limit.

When I arrived it began to rain. I was allocated a pitch next to a lively couple who had created a spider's web of ties between their tent and a nearby tree. They both wore sunglasses and danced to ambient rave music in their tenty porch as the rain beat down. Their hats were hilarious and very 'his and hers'. It seemed they were determined to have a bloody good time - no matter what was thrown at them - even if their tent blew away.

The pitch itself was deluxe and was positioned right beside the lake. I had my own EHC, water tap and a picnic bench. To launch my paddle board I had around twenty steps from the van to the pebbly beach. I was so pleased. The view was astounding because perilous peaks rose up around the lakes and swathes of cloud decorated them. It was marvellous! I was desperate for a paddle; however, my gut said wait. I knew the weather could change in a minute out there and had to be careful. I turned on the mobile data and checked the weather forecast. What a surprise! Another storm was on its way. Time for a nap!

Between showers I took a bit of a wander around the site because it was a working farm and saw the strangest thing. A cow mounted another cow and in the momentum drove the other cow forward into the cow shed. In the throes of the action the mountee cow banged its head on the top of the shed door and mooed. I don't think that was your average mounting, mating tactic. After the cow shed incident, I checked out the showers and washing-up areas. They were all lovely, organised and clean. On the stroll back I stopped off at the onsite café to be greeted by the lovely owner who was lively, chatty and stocked all sorts of gluten-free and alternative milks. I couldn't have wished for anything better.

Well I couldn't help myself and ordered an almond hot chocolate and a gluten-free biscuit. We ended up chatting about the site and the fact she was lactose intolerant which had resulted in gut-wrenching stomach ache after drinking far too many lattes. The result was she realised there was a campsite market for alternative milks to accommodate those who were gluten-free. Even on the themed food evenings she made sure she catered for intolerances. I found that amazing and was so pleased. She asked where I pitched. I pointed towards the lake. She smiled, 'The couple next to you are regulars. I think you will get on well. You might be interested to hear their story…' she said with wink, which felt very mysterious.

She gestured towards the lake. 'I would make your way back now because that there front is going to hit in around ten minutes. It is rolling down the hill, will hit the lake and rampage towards the site. It is going to be brutal,' she said. 'Oh and make sure you secure or put away anything that could be blown away.'
She knew what she was talking about. She saw the conditions on a daily basis.

CHAPTER 37

THE STICK IN THE MUD

That afternoon a downpour ensued which was so intense that the nearby hills appeared to transform into waterfalls as the water descended to the lake. Talk about a stick in the mud situation, well it was more of a van in the mud scenario. It might not be obvious to some that vans are heavy vehicles. We live in England, which is prone to unpredictable weather and deluges of rain. Where there are vans, grass and rain there is mud. That is something to be very aware of, especially when the pitch is beside a hill and in a dip. I have special tracks that can be placed under the wheels to get the van moving in muddy conditions. I learned that lesson by watching (from a distance) a couple who had parked in a bit of a gully on a site which became a mud bath. Basically there had been rain for days and that rain washed down the hill into a bit of dip. That dip did have a nice view and the vaneers concerned must have thought they had found a prime location with an unobstructed view, with no other vans in close proximity. Unfortunately, the couple soon discovered why the area was vacant.

After endless downpours, the rainwater ran down the surrounding slopes and turned the area they were parked into a bit of a swamp. What often happens in such circumstances is that people remain in the comfort of their vans and attempt to sit out the weather. Of course no one knows how long a downpour will last or how much water multiple cloudbursts will create. That time the rain went on for three days with showers on the fourth and fifth. The thing is when you have wet weather gear the conditions don't really bother you. You just go out anyway and that is why I always take waterproofs, walking boots and wellies.

Anyway, I digressed, so the couple sat out the inclement weather and came to the end of their vancation. When they went to drive off they made an unfortunate discovery: the ground was sodden. When the wheels turned, the mud spattered everywhere. The more they tried to drive the deeper they sunk. The thing was they were determined. What made it worse was that the lady got out to see if she could direct her partner. In doing so, he spun the wheels and coated her in mud spattering. I don't think that did much for the relationship because there wasn't a lot of laughing but plenty of swearing.

Now what is wonderful about the camping community is that people help each other. There are plenty of vangels around, as I call them. Vangels are those who happily help others. On that occasion there was an abundance of vangels, so numerous friendly campers got involved in the van liberation. Some took cardboard over, others bought tracks, and we all got involved. I can tell you trying to push a large mobile home from the depths of a mud-pit is a challenge. With around twenty of us, all manner of constructed platform, and a bit of luck, we managed to free up the mobile hippopotamus and get it to the main track. It was really quite a united feat. In the end we were all coated in mud, had waded through mud and had really had to give the van a real bit of shoulder.

The couple were so relieved when they started moving. In fact the mud-spattered lady almost cried with emotion. That was a turning point for me and I invested in two plastic tracks. That evening I ended up chatting with some of the other campers. It turned out quite a few had been in similar situations and had learned to scope the area to avoid mud-inducing incidents. Some of the campers mentioned they had used their van foot mats, cardboard, blankets and even sleeping bags to get out of mud-terrifying situations. The blankets and sleeping bags (those with finer materials) were shredded and ruined. Obviously there is a bit of a lesson there and it made it understandable why many of the larger vehicles chose hard standing pitches to avoid such situations.

That afternoon the sky descended into a deeply murky grey. It appeared to be conspiring with the elements to brutalise those on the edge of the lake. 'That storm is building!' said Shelley, my neighbour. Her chap, Pete, got up, went over to their tent and tied additional guide ropes from the tent to the tree with one eye closed. All the while he stumbled left and then right. In securing the tent he tied his fingers into the knots a couple of times. When he had finished the elaborate spidery-web arrangement he returned.

'That cloud doesn't just look like rain. Look at how the edges of the cloud are lifted. That is big winds too.' He was clearly concerned because a bit of canvas between them and the inclement weather meant they were unlikely to come out winners. His wife studied her weather app as she sipped some more gin. 'We are about to be hit by a monster,' she said glancing at us both and turning her phone screen towards us. 'Make the most of it now because the forecast says fifty mile an hour winds and wintery showers.'

Nuts! I glanced across at the tent beside me. They were inside and had not ventured out. Beside them a large van with its awning up, pop-top popped and a privacy tent erected kept to themselves. I glanced at the squiffy pair, 'Do you think I should warn them?'

They nodded half-heartedly. I went to get up and heard the zip of the tent beside me open.

'Hi…' I said 'It's about to get very stormy. I hope your pegs are firmly in.' The two ladies, with short hair and a lovely pup sighed, 'We can't get the pegs deep because the ground has rock below it.' The pair glanced up at the sky and appeared concerned.

'That is why we created the spider's web of different lines to the tree. That way we don't blow off!' said the neighbour beside me with a lovely slur. The squiffy couple fell into laughter.

'You always blow off!' Shelley cried. 'So do you,' her husband responded. They then laughed and laughed until they coughed.

The lady couple smirked and glanced at me curiously. The Gin-a-ling-a-ding-dongs were absolutely hilarious. With the storm gaining momentum, we were neighbourly and helped the two ladies bash in their pegs. Shelley, the lady ginster seemed to be missing her target; however, she was giving it some welly nonetheless.

In the meantime, I went over to the other van. I didn't think they were in because there was no answer when I knocked. Actually maybe they were there but chose not to answer. I wrote a note and placed it on the handle. *It might be worth taking in the awning because we have fifty five mile an hour winds on their way.* Hopefully they would get that little note in time. As I walked away the little blighter blew past. I realised nothing that could be blown away would remain in place. What could you do?

It is funny how you feel the edge of a storm as it arrives. The early gusts make a recognisance of the area and prepare the route for the full gusts arrival. In less than twenty minutes we watched the wall of weather descend upon us. It was incredible to observe how the storm literally trampled across the lake. When it was close we all dived in our vans and tents. We braced ourselves because something epic was about to take place.

The golf ball sized hailstones bounced in the same way as ping-pong balls when they hit the ground and the van. The ping-pongy assault sounded as though a group of paintballers had unleashed a paintballing extravaganza on the campsite. Shortly after the wind blustered us into an inner-van/tent shake. Ping-ponging, blustering and gusting proceeded with vengeance.

At the same time I continued to listen to the book *Catch 22* as I gazed out at the view. The lake formed waves and the tents either side were indented when the wind overpowered them. I laid gazing out of the window, put some meditation music on and drifted into sleep.

I peered out of the window at around eight that evening. The sozzled couple's tent beside me was still intact. Unfortunately the tent with the two ladies and pup looked as though it had been ripped from its pegs. Half of it was still firm but the entrance area flapped with each gust. The van beyond them was lacking a privacy tent because that tent had blown away. The pop-top didn't look as though it stood a chance and was preparing to take a tour of nearby trees.

There was something so fascinating about how we all reacted to the same storm. It seems to be a common theme: how each person is affected by the same circumstances in a different way. I sat inside Blossom and wound down the window on the sheltered side of the van. I cooked my dinner and took in the view. The weather wasn't going to change. I was glad I had a porta potty because I didn't need to leave the van to go to the bathroom.

There wasn't much a person could do other than read, listen to audio, watch a DVD, do handy-crafts, colour stuff in or do nothing. I decided to have an early night. If the weather calmed then paddle boarding first thing would be wonderful. That night the weather took a turn for the worse. Bucketing downpours descended upon us. I wondered how my neighbours would respond. As I prepared my bed and de-ruckled my sleeping bag, I heard rave music and looked out. My drunken colleagues both wore pork-pie hats and rave danced around their pitch waving fluorescent sticks and lit sparklers. They filmed each other on their phones, laughed like delighted children, and pulled some rather odd dance moves. That was a surprise!

The neighbours on the other side remained inside the remains of the canopy. There was no stirring just silence and no light. Something about the different responses provided an insight. The unfortunate truth was as much as the storm was gusting, it was about to up its game!

That night was like sleeping in a bladeless blender. Gusts, blasts, shaking and pounding rain. I slept well considering. What I find odd is that you are aware of the conditions yet you manage to sleep. Admittedly I wondered how the ladies in the tent would fare. What would happen to the other vaneers on site? Quite a number hadn't un-popped-tops or taken in their awnings. There was likely to be a storm massacre by morning.

At about four in the morning a silence descended. Tranquillity unfolded and by dawn absolute calm filled the air. The glassy lake didn't reveal a ripple. What's more, the weather seemed to stabilise. When such moments occur I take the opportunity. I quickly launched my paddle board, made my way to the centre of the lake and glanced back at the campsite. It had been demolished! A lot of the tents were displaced with shredded areas scattered around them. A few of the ripped awnings accompanied privacy tents up in trees. If you wanted privacy it was there with a view!

I made my way back to shore after a serene paddle. Numerous vans attempted to drive out of the mud. Many had picked pitches that became boggy and sodden when the rain transformed into mini-rivers that surged down the hills. No one wanted to remain stuck in the mud, so they attempted to move and ended up driving themselves deeper. The more they accelerated the deeper the wheels became entrenched. As mentioned previously, everyone got involved. Groups of vaneers gathered and attempted to help each other. All the while mud sprayed everywhere and spattered anyone who passed by. There were times when so much mud was being sprayed that the situation could be misconstrued as a mud wrestling convention.

I made my way up the beach and decided I would get my 'tracks' and take them over to those who were stranded. That idea was thwarted because I discovered my lady neighbours arguing upon my return. One wanted to go home while the other wanted to stay. It turned out that during the night the rain had gushed through their tent and soaked the pair of them. They tried to deal with it but enough was enough and they ended up driving to a hotel. The extra cost bothered them and their pup was anxious.

On the other side of the van the dancing drunken dandies happily indulged in a good fry up. The dance of the sausage accompanied rave music. The impaled sausages were waved in the air in time to the beat and around each other's faces. The pair giggled, jiggled and raved with their sausages.

The ladies beside me packed up after a heated discussion. Their departure made sense because the weather for the next few days was changeable and they couldn't endure another sleepless night. The sausage-wielding couple beside me shrugged. We said goodbye and then I asked the couple about their dance the previous night. 'It was a rain rave... We are currently doing the sausage sway... The rain rave generally begins when the weather is extreme. We have a change of clothes in the tent to deal with the soakage.'

'I think that's brilliant and love that attitude'. I replied.

'Well, we have decided to make the most of every moment because Pete here is terminal and has around three months left on the planet. We decided to make the best memories and live the best life because you always want more time. No matter what the weather we make the most of it because when you are pushing up the daisies you need all weather to make your seeds bloom.' Shelley said pretending to be a daisy.

You know when something hits you so hard – a side winder. The couple had limited time and were living their fullest now. They made the most of everything and were hilarious. Yet behind the scenes there was a dark cloud. It made me very reflective and made me ask myself the question – does the weather have to affect adVANture? Or… do you simply make the most of it by having the right kit?

My thoughts were interrupted by a slurred request. 'Oh talking of enjoying everything. Would you mind coming paddle boarding with me because I don't want to go alone? I don't trust myself with a paddle board, a huge lake and changeable weather.' Shelley said even though it was clear she was shit-faced!

How could I refuse after such a conversation?

CHAPTER 38

THE OTHER NEIGHBOURS AND HOW THEY DEALT WITH STORMS

A large glass of gin was clasped in my lively neighbour's hand at six in the morning. She had said she would like to join me for an early morning paddle board. She swaggered in my direction with a gin grin expression. In all honesty the likelihood of her being able to stand on a board was quite remote, so I suggested she take out her kayak. When she talked she garbled her words. In the end I suggested it might be better that her and I go for a paddle in the afternoon. Maybe she should have a bit more sleep, some carbs and some water. Even in her inebriated state, she realised it was in her best interest and had taken the 'hair of the dog' so that she could come out on the water. I made a few jokes about being drunk and in control of a floatation vessel. Although, the truth was, she was definitely still drunk. Going out on a lake with such changeable conditions, with someone who was not well practiced at being on the water, drunk and not terribly fit was foolish to say the least. It could endanger us both.

In the end she took the sleeping suggestion well and dived into her tent and onto her blow-up bed. From what I can gather, her 'smash down' resulted in her husband being launched in the air because he swore while he was elevated, I then heard him bounce into his bed. What a way to be woken – by finding yourself suspended in the air – oh that is familiar, that was my van acquisition turning point. Anyway there was a hearty laugh from my neighbour, which may have woken up most of the people in the area. With that in mind, I launched and headed out to the centre of the lake with my coffee and dark chocolate. It was peaceful there, the sky was blue, the mountains had wafts of cloud draped over them and it was all perfectly reflected in stillness. I sat for a while in the quiet and just enjoyed not rushing, not having to be anywhere and not talking. It was bliss. I was completely relaxed and in nature. It would be the complete contrast to what was going to be quite a gincident later on.

At four o'clock my neighbour burst from her tent. She was energised, ready and still quite sozzled. She had pumped up her kayak, made a picnic, filled a litre water bottle with gin and tonic and was 'ready to rumble' - those were her words. There was no way I would be able to fob her off. She was going on the water and that was it! Her husband, who was also gin grinning, sat with his book looking pleased. 'She has been looking forward to this all day, and I can read my book in peace.'

Well what do you do? If I didn't go with her then she would go alone... and that was probably more dangerous.

Well things didn't get off to a terribly good start. The word elegance did not apply to how she entered the kayak and for a while she floundered face down. I focused on arranging my board and paddle. At the same time I kept an eye on her. Finally she was sorted and began to paddle out. I followed and sat cross-legged on my board because I was concerned that she may well ram me which would knock me in. She didn't, but there were a few unexpected meanderings. Anyway, I directed her along the shore and kept her in a relatively shallow area with a short distance to the beach. I also made sure she had her lifejacket on… She did. Anyway, I stood up and glanced at her, she seemed to be struggling. I then realised she had her kayak back to front. Yep it was possible because it was a blow-up canoe.

'Erm… is you kayak back to front?' I asked.

A huge hearty laugh and 'Yep… I thought it was hard work!'

'Shall we go over to the shore? We can stop for a snack, sort out the kayak and then have an easy paddle,' I suggested.

Well, we made it ashore to an area with lots of sheep. She stumbled up the beach and sat in a sheep turd. I didn't know what to say… Did I tell her? Or did we leave it? In the end I mentioned there was something on her bottom. She found it hilarious. We then sat and had a bit of a picnic. She wanted me to share her snacks – she had made a bit of a smorgasboard. It was lovely. She sat beaming with delight. 'I love this… WE are on an adventure.'

It seemed that her and her husband visited that site every year now and loved the lake, especially the views. She had bought a kayak a while ago and had no one to go with. She admitted she was not confident enough to go alone. So this little paddle was an absolute joy for her... She told me how she was a chef in a care home and how she planned to retire in five years. She said that during Covid half of the care home had been wiped out. It turned out, only she and one other did not get the virus. She put that down to the gin. Her colleague put it down to vodka. I put it down to random illness roulette.

Anyway, she finished off the olives, meat and cheese, downed some of her gin mix, and quickly climbed in her kayak brimming with confidence. So much so she started paddling across the lake. I wasn't quite so fast and noticed that the lake ferry was sailing across the centre of the lake. It was too far away to collide with her, yet something about being with someone inebriated on a floatation device, a ferry heading in their direction and a huge lake unsettled me. In fact my gut turned.

Shelley was in a rhythm and now she had the kayak the right way round she was giving it some welly. She was definitely making headway. She saw a beach across the lake with a forest area. She called over her shoulder – 'I am heading towards that beach. I need a pee!'

Great!

I followed with a lovely rhythm and a glide. I glanced over at the ferry, if I could keep her occupied then it would mean that she would not cross its path, which would be a relief. Shelley reached the beach and rammed into it with the kayak. There was a loud grating sound as the bottom of the Kayak collided with the shingle. Once jammed on shore, she used a roll-out technique and scrambled to her knees. She then swaggered over to the nearby trees to have a 'lady break'. Once she was done she sauntered back smiling. The ferry had just passed. I sat on my board just offshore and watched the rather random contortions used to climb back into the kayak. It seemed that Shelley was so consumed in warping her way in the kayak that she did not pay attention to anything else. She launched and began to paddle just as the ferry's bow waves undulated in our direction. I turned my board and sat realising that there was going to be a bouncy unfolding.

'Shelley, turn your kayak into the waves and ride over them,' I called.

'What waves?' she replied with a slur.

Too late. Shelley tipped over and was washed ashore. The waves washed over her and withdrew, leaving her floundering on the beach. She was soaked and laid screaming with delight. She found it hilarious. That is what I loved about her... everything was funny. She sat with her legs splayed and gathered herself. 'That was sooo fun!'

For a moment she gathered her breath, checked the kayak was the right way round and glanced across the lake to see if there were any more waves. She climbed in and her body obviously deflated. She glanced over at me and said, 'I am tired now. I haven't done exercise for years.'

'We will take it slow and go back...' I responded, she looked like she needed a nap.

She smiled, 'This is the best day ever! Wait until I tell Pete!'

We created a nice rhythm, said hello to a few other paddle boarders and went ashore. Shelley carried her small kayak up the beach and went over to Pete.

'Such an adventure! I loved it! She finished off her gin and tonic. She then grinned at us both. 'I think it's time for a nap.'

She came over to me and gave me a huge cuddle. 'Thank you so much. We will have to do that again... '

Hmmm.

She then started to nod forward. I wondered if she was a narcoleptic but I think the gin, the excitement and the exercise wiped her out. She suddenly woke up, threw her arms around me again and gave me another cuddle. She then looked me in the eyes and said 'BED!' With that she turned, opened her tent flap and launched herself on the blow-up bed. It made a loud raspberry sound. I then heard a snore. Pete lifted his eyes from his book. 'We have seven blow-up beds… They don't last…' With that he smiled, I heard some more snores and realised it was time to go and lay in my hammock.

When I think about the Gin-a-ling-a-ding-dong couple who camped beside me and their attitude to life, I realised there was a common theme among many of the people I had met. Most had had some kind of wake-up call which catapulted them into action. One lady I met paddling on the lake had lost her wife to cancer and she was only forty-three. She had thrown caution to the wind – sold up, bought a van and re-trained as a landscape gardener. She had a beautiful van and lived as a garden designing nomad. Her dog accompanied her on her trips as well as on her paddle board. She said at times her life was lonely, but it would have been worse sitting in her old home without the love of her life.

At the other end of the scale were the Gin-a-ling-a-ding-dongs who danced in the rain, made the most of everything and lived life as though it was a constant party because you never know when party-time would be raided or ruined. Both had arrived at the same conclusion – do it now! Don't take life seriously. Don't put life off. Do what you love your way. In so many books they make out it is suddenly easy if you do this… this or this… That is just a marketing technique. Life wasn't easy for either of them, yet they made the most of it. It was their attitude to the struggles and their grief that was impressive. It is interesting to consider how annoying life has to get before one makes a change. How mundane does a job have to become? How badly treated or fed-up do you have to be in a relationship? Obviously we all have the desire to be safe but how safe and for how long? What did that need for safety, combined with a fear of change, make a person miss out on? Did there really have to be a wake-up call to force a person to truly live and enjoy? Did death have to stare a person in the face for them to appreciate life?

Admittedly not everyone can just chuck in the towel and take off but isn't it odd that we feel we have to chuck in the towel? Why don't work places provide opportunity to have regular adventures or lifestyle/travel experiences? Of course not everyone desires adventures. The thing is there is no opportunity for those that do - not terribly clever if you ask me… How about an adventure break rather than a sabbatical? An adventure break is where people take some time out to experience and return to work a better person. I find the work-factory mentality somewhat archaic now, especially in an era where we will be running out of good human resources and employers will have to compete for good staff.

The thing is many people can work remotely. If people desire to live their best lives now because we have climate change, endless volatility in financial markets and wars… why would anyone not want to live fully rather than sit in front of screens for hours on end…?

There has to be a better way. I hope that taking time out will provide insight. It may well reveal that I like routines and the mundane. The thing is whatever one learns, it is worth learning to live the best way you can in the now and be present with all that you experience rather than rush through it like an 'experience treadmill'.

All of those thoughts stampeded through my mind as I watched the Gin-a-ling-a-ding-dongs pack up and prepare to go home. The truth was he was about to start to decline. Shelley was going to support him throughout. At least they had created some brilliant memories to get them through the next phase… The question that rose in my mind was how do I enjoy life more? At that point of the trip, I had loved every moment and each day seemed to get better and better as I met more and more people and heard their stories.

CHAPTER 39

OFF THE TOURIST TRACK

I felt quite reluctant to leave the Lake District. Even though the weather had been doubtful, I had met some amazing people and had some beautiful paddles. In addition, I was venturing further into the unknown. When most people talk about visiting Scotland in a van they mention the North Coast 500. From what I gather, it has become commercialised and every Tom, Dick and Mary are following that route. The purpose of my trip was to be away from people, to get some peace and quiet, and spend time in nature recharging. The last thing I fancied was following a NC500 crowd. So with that in mind, I decided to make my way around Scotland and decided Galloway was somewhere I would like to explore. I had read that the Scottish Forestry Commission had a new scheme where you could park overnight in their carparks. I thought I would do that the first couple of nights and then go properly wild and wild camp. It was all very exciting albeit a little bit frightening because if werewolves were going to be anywhere then they would be lurking in the Scottish forests.

The journey from the Lake District was a long one, although it was relatively easy because I left so early in the morning. Thank goodness I departed at the crack of dawn because there was a rather large roundabout near Glasgow that I had to circumnavigate a few times until I managed to get on the correct road. I think it had around ten branches and multiple lanes. Admittedly I was kind to myself regarding that roundabout expedition because it is very easy to get angry and frustrated which makes me feel a complete wombat. I took a few stops on the way but something in me just wanted to get to Galloway.

When someone described the trees as dripping with lichen, I thought that maybe they had sniffed too many daisies whilst drinking gin. I was wrong. That particular forestry location in Scotland blew me away in terms of lichen levels. I have never seen anything like it or inhaled air so crisp, green and fresh. The description 'dripping with lichen' was an understatement. Think of the hairiest beard you can imagine, multiply that by five and now turn it a vibrant green. Take that green beardedness and coat every tree in the forest in it. That still does not do the lichen levels any justice.

Now, as I mentioned before, I was on a mission to find complete solitude in nature. I wanted to be away from everyone, and Wi-Fi, and immerse myself in the depths of Mother Nature. Well I found my ideal place and I will not write the name here because I want to return there. In the meantime I hope that the place is not discovered and ruined. Yes it is in Scotland and it is off the beaten track. Admittedly I did see other vaneers in and around the area. They were being relatively discreet and were very respectful in terms of rubbish. Nothing left, no trace… Which is how it should be.

Anyway back to the forest. A few days prior I had met a couple who were on their return from Scotland. As with all van-versations you find yourself sharing insights, stories, locations and lessons. The couple had been wild camping in various forests and mentioned they had been to a place where the trees were 'dripping in lichen'. I did smile to myself when the film *Ghostbusters* popped into my mind and I had an image of green slime... I kept that to myself. The thing is there is a fine line between wanting to experience such natural wonders and by staying within it, one is affecting it. If we could all float around on magic carpets, not trampling flowers or scraping the micro-environments then maybe I would feel better about disclosing such wondrous places exist. The thing is this place was astounding and was not on the famous North Coast 500.

In truth, as much as I would love to do the NC500, it has become over-popular and crowded. The result was that it became packed, rubbish was strewn and locals were aggravated. I don't like that game, so prefer to be away from the throngs. I wanted to make my own way, with my own path to places that had not been over-popularised. I enjoyed plotting my route, taking my time and discovering that there were 'dark sky areas' where the galaxies could be viewed.

I spent my afternoon parking up ipn different areas and having little mini-explores. I intended to do that until six in the evening, which was when you could go to the carpark and pitch up. Well I was so involved in my little explores that I didn't notice the time. It was suddenly eight o'clock. I drove for thirty minutes to my sleeping destination of choice. The phenomenal forestry location was in the middle of nowhere and renowned for its sky clarity. In that remote part of the forest there was a forestry carpark where I discovered only around six other vans in an area that could take thirty. The other vaneers were respectful and were parked as far away from each other as was possible. I noticed a gritted area behind some bushes where I parked up and gazed into the night. There were hoots of owls, and what I assume to be bats because dark flying creatures passed over the moon. There was scurrying in the hedges which could have been anything – of course the mind always imagines murderers and monsters. That kind of imagination always catches me off-guard.

I set up my fold-out chair and gazed up at the sky – it was so clear with no fluorescent light which meant you could see the Milky Way. At the same time the air was so fresh and cooled by the forest. That tinge of green lichen created a crisp aroma which filled the air, lifted the soul and cleansed the lungs. A sense of silence, solitude and absolute serenity permeated my being. My soul sang and I felt an absolute connection combined with awe and bliss. In that moment I realised that my trip was something that was going to change me on all levels. I had never felt such stillness, calm and peace – I had made space for it and followed my intuition; something I have ignored in times gone by. The reward was witnessing the forest, the Milky Way and a sky so vast and so clear that it was almost incomprehensible.

I stayed outside until eleven, which is way past my bedtime but I could not stop admiring the sky, its vastness and how clear all the stars were. I knew that I would wake up at first light but for once I would not feel sleep-deprived because being there recharged me, ignited me and enlivened me. It was different to getting up to an alarm, instead I was waking up to nature and following natural rhythms.

The following morning there were clouds, a red rising sun and the fresh fragrance of nature, the forest and lichen. At five in the morning I did not bother with coffee instead I made my way along a path into the depths of the forest and allowed my cells to absorb nature's nutrients. I then did Tai Chi and lifted my energy to a new heightened state. In that moment the world resonated at a higher frequency. I was blessed to reside in a body, in that space, in that time and in that place. My heart was vibrant and I was filled with absolute awe… I felt truly alive as I gazed at the beams of light illuminating the lichen – nature was astounding!

I could have spent hours there, just being and I probably did spend a couple of hours completely immersed in the details of the flora and fauna. Time evaporated and I wasn't bothered because I did not have to be anywhere doing anything. I could flow with the day and simply enjoy. There was no rush, no schedule and no expectation. Something I had not realised affected me so deeply. It was then I realised the level of contrast between my life in technology and how I felt in that moment. I purposely made sure I was present with every part of that experience because I desired to impress it into the depths of my being, so that in less ecstatic times I could reach back to it and use it to enliven myself. I am so very glad I did.

The rest of the day flowed, I spent time in the forest and sighed when it was time to leave. The rule with the carpark stays is that it is for only one night. So, I had to move on. It was a shame, but that place was somewhere I intended to return to in the future. The bright side was I was about to move on to an equally inspirational location.

CHAPTER 40

LOCH GNOME

I had read about Clatteringshaws on one of the *Women With Van's* social media sites. It seemed the ideal place to park for the night with a lovely view of the loch. Essentially the overnight carpark sat beside a café. There was a phenomenal view; although it was close to a road. It seemed that motorbikes took great joy in giving it some welly along the road and creating a roaring ruckus. I have to admit after staying in some places of silence and solitude, I really noticed the sound of the motor bikes. On top of that there was a group of chaps that had hired Porsches and Ferraris. They were doing a fast car navigation of Scotland. They turned up in the carpark in the afternoon because they were stopping for a snack and a pee. They all appeared very pleased with themselves in their fast cars making engine roaring noises.

I watched the other vaneers, approximately about six of us, study the fast car brigade. It was like watching two completely different species gaging each other – very much tortoise versus hares. The fast car brigade were racing around Scotland and their focus was going fast, taking the bends and travelling in car manoeuvrability. The vaneers were at the other end of the scale: they were taking it slow with their 'shells' on their backs. They could stop, rest and luxuriate in the view any time they wished and of course there was always a napportunity.

I did make it away from the carpark and went for a wander past the café and beside the lake. I found a couple of viewpoints and sat on a bench. I took the opportunity to journal my experiences and became quite emersed in writing. My focus was broken by a little boy of around seven and a girl of around six who said 'Excuse me... What are you doing?'

I told them I was writing in my journal. They seemed confused. 'Why would you do that?'

'It is a pleasure to write,' I replied. 'Where are your parents?' I asked, somewhat concerned.

They pointed down the hill. The next thing I knew a group of fifteen surrounded me and were watching me write my journal. It felt somewhat weird. Finally one of the group said 'Are you a writer?'

I said 'Yes. I am. I have lots of books out on Amazon.'

He looked puzzled pulled out his phone and went on Amazon. He asked what my name was. I told him my pen name and he looked it up. His eyes nearly blew out of his head. 'You really are a writer. Lots of books.' He then passed the phone around to all of his family. The whole group just stood in silence gawping at me. I now know how zoo animals feel and realised I did not like the attention; which is why I keep my writing to myself. Anyway, he took his phone back and bought five of my books there and then.

'I have bought the children's books,' he said with a smile. He then crouched down and took his children in his arms. 'This lady writes books. She writes for children too. We will read some of her books on our holiday...'

The children grinned and continued staring.

'Can I touch you?' the little boy asked. I nodded. He came over patted my knee and ran off giggling. The whole family laughed awkwardly, gawped at me some more and then realised that I might want to carry on writing. The group shifted awkwardly and said 'We are from Birmingham.'

'Oh I hope you have a lovely holiday... Where are you off to?' I asked.

'We have a holiday cottage near a castle in Douglas. Right by a castle,' the mother replied with a huge grin.

'That will be lovely for the kiddiwinks...'

They all nodded and smiled. There was that awkward silence again and finally they shuffled away. 'Byeeee!'

I think what was odd for me was that I had found a bench away from everyone with my great plan to seek solitude and... then I end up surrounded by a group of people. I had no idea how that was possible. It did remind me of how happy I am that I have kept anonymous all these years of writing. I really don't like the attention at all.

I finished writing in my journal and added in that little experience. I then took a stroll to a pine area where I ran into a couple of ladies whose dog decided I was its new best friend. Now I love dogs… Really love dogs, so I played with the dog and almost forgot the humans were there. Of course a conversation ensued and we discussed how calm the atmosphere was there. The lady owner was travelling with the pup in her van and had met up with another lady who was studying permaculture on the same course as her. The pair told me all about how pine trees have an aroma which is calming. They had both given up professional careers in business to study sustainability and permaculture. They were both passionate about their subject and were both in their mid-forties. One said it was definitely a mid-life crisis. The other said it was a mid-life learning and awakening. The lady with the van said she was so pleased to be able to hook up through Wi-Fi and study while vanning it up… I loved their attitude and adaptability.

After a bit more of a ramble and taking the time to enjoy the surroundings, I headed back to the café and… there it was: a gnome. It was dressed in yellow and had a red hat. There were fairy doors on nearby trees and a few other gnomes dotted around the area. I couldn't believe it. There were no signs or anything suggesting that we were in another gnome land. I did smile to myself. Gnome Sanctuary escapades had become reality. So I took some fun pictures and sent them to Teresa.

When I arrived back at the carpark I ended up chatting to a couple in their late sixties who gave me a tour of their van. They had retired and were now adVANturing. Their van was a high-top with two single beds, a shower, a proper kitchen and a loo. It was a lovely van. We ended up chatting about places and quite quickly another couple joined us. The chap strolled over and said 'You were staying at the same place as us yesterday… I recognise your van… Could we see the interior?'

I glanced across the carpark. That couple had a lovely new mobile home.

'Of course but it is a tiddler… in comparison to yours,' I replied.

He said that was why he was curious. Well I showed him the interior and the other couple came for a peek. They were stunned by how 'efficient' such a small van was. I had the bed set up already and thank goodness it was tidy. What had made them curious was how stealthy it was and yet they had seen me at the other pitch merrily pulling out my chairs and table and looking very comfortable. They were stunned that I was spending a few months in such a small space. I didn't think of it like that because I only really spend time inside the van when it is raining or if I am sleeping. The rest of the time I am usually outside… So a small van worked well. I think it would have been tricky if I had adVANtured with my ex because of the bed width. We shared single beds previously, meaning we had slept in a single bed because he 'accidentally' booked a single room at hotels. He had been super impressed by a hotel bargain but had not realised the single bed situation. He assumed all hotels had doubles... Anyway that was another story. In the end the group got together, arranged our fold-out chairs and watched the sun set over the lake. There was gin, wine, cider, and being that I am extreme – fizzy water. I do sometimes like a cider but only on occasion and that was not an occasion where I felt the urge to drink.

I have to say it was a lovely evening with some fabulous vaneers. The chap with the mobile home and his wife had been all over Europe. They had retired at fifty and decided they wanted to live fully. They shipped their kids out of their house, decided to buy a mobile home and explored all that they could for as long as they could. They had had some rather interesting sticky jams on some of the roads in Wales and on Dartmoor. We discussed having to reverse miles down stone-walled lanes and all of the awkward places to pass with steep edges. I sat there with this lovely group of people and thought how wonderful it was that five strangers could have such an open chat and then... two more joined us. They had set up in the corner and thought they would come over and say hello. Two more fold-out chairs later and we were discussing wild camping. We had all noticed how quite often when you attempt to park alone another van will pull up at the same layby. We all assumed they were thinking safety in numbers or... Wow they have found a lovely view to wake up to.

It's at times like that you feel completely connected. You realise there are others who share the same travel passion and sense of adventure. What's more, to meet people that are open, honest, friendly and inviting is a joy.

We all watched the sun set. The temperature dropped and Jill said she wanted to do a bit of crochet before bed. That tickled me: 'I want to fit in a bit of crochet...' It was said like it was the most normal thing in the world. At that moment it was.

CHAPTER 41

WILD AND SLOW

On the way to Loch Lomond I stayed at a couple of other wild locations, which I am not going to disclose. I also stayed at a very quiet location close to the village of Drymen, beside the West Highlands Way. My time there was relaxing, involved walking or exploring nearby forests. It wasn't terribly eventful so I am not going to write too much. What I will say is the weather was lovely. Napping was glorious and the rustling trees were fabulous. I didn't really talk to many people and discovered a lack of vegetables in the local shops. My food highlight was fish and chips at the pub in Drymen. The time there was perfect because there was a distinct lack of doing. Which was precisely what I needed before going to Loch Lomond.

Loch Lomond has a certain atmosphere. It is expansive, calming and inspirational - precisely what I needed. I have to admit that spending time there recharged me. What I realised (the more I reflected) is how I had been crying out for solitude, silence and serenity. I managed to achieve that by going paddle boarding at five-thirty in the morning and paddling out to the middle of the lake. Some might consider that stupid. Maybe foolish, being out in the middle of a lake alone. However, I always gage where I go according to whether I can swim back to shore. I note the wind speeds, wind direction and cloud formations. When it comes to rivers and seas I check the tides too.

On this particular morning I decided to go for a bit of a paddling jaunt. I had coffee, dark chocolate and water in my survival pack. I paddled out to the middle of the lake, and even though I had paddled for eight hours most days, I felt a pang of fear. It was odd and definitely triggered a lot of thoughts. The thing is I suddenly realised how deep that water was. Something about the concept of descending into the depths made me fearful. What was interesting was the reality that I was sitting on the surface of a well inflated paddle board.

For a long time I sat in silence gazing at wisps of clouds drifting over nearby mountains. I watched the sun rise and sparkle as it emerged for the new day. There was no sound of traffic, no people running around screaming… just silence, solitude and serenity. The moment expanded and all my cells rejoiced – finally, some proper expansive quiet. I sipped my coffee and ate some chocolate while I took in the view. I then decided to paddle across to a small island with a beach that was directly opposite the campsite. It reminded me of the film *The Beach*.

After about five minutes I waded across the shore and admired ancient trees, some beautiful rock formations and a spectacular view of the loch surrounded by mountains. I gazed back at the campsite and felt blessed that I had made such a journey to Scotland and was now standing on an uninhibited island in the middle of a loch. All of that because I had invested in Blossom. I would never have been able to make such a trip had I had to pay for hotels. Instead, Blossom had been both my chariot and my home from home. I sat for a moment pondering the unexpected fear, how such natural beauty rejuvenated one's soul and how many people fear solitude. I loved it.

I went for an explore around the island because I was curious what was on the other side. Well it turns out there were more islands beyond that one and I could see the other side of the loch. There was so much water to explore in all directions. It was then I realised that I would need to stay a bit longer and explore a bit more. I have to say I had no clue how much I would love the raw Scottish nature and the fresh feeling it provided.

I felt a pang of hunger and decided to return to the site. I would most definitely be out on the board throughout the day and evening. In the end I spent eight hours paddling, which most definitely justified my diet of meat, veg and a bit of chocolate. What was funny was that some of the other vaneers asked how long I paddled for. I said around eight hours. They were stunned, the thing is it didn't take effort because the beauty of the place energised me. Admittedly, if someone was not a regular paddler I would advise against spending so long on the water, but I couldn't help it. It was as if there was a magnetic pull that kept calling me back. Maybe it was the ease of which I could be away from people and noise or the serene reflections that appeared on the surface of the water. Whatever it was, I couldn't get enough of it... I literally fell in love with the location. I have to admit I spent days and days at the site. I read, paddled, slept and gazed at the landscape. I think I could have spent months there. By that point I felt fully rejuvenated. I met plenty of people and am always fascinated by how people's paths cross, along with the stories they share.

During my stay I met two sisters who were very different. One had decked out her micro-camper, while the other one was adamant about being wild camp efficient and would meet her sister in locations and set up her tarp. She was hard core because she was running the trail while her sister was vanning. The sister with the van loved her van approach because she gradually made her way to each stop. For her, she was making little journeys with the support of a sister at the end. Once she had set up, she would walk in the direction her sister was coming from. She would then walk the last part with her sister who may have been running for a few hours by that point. It was quite a well-co-ordinated arrangement and one that worked for them. They were going to cover a lot of the Highlands Way, and more. What was nice about the trip was they were taking their time and both had put work on hold to spend time with each other – to really get to know and understand each other. When they arrived at Loch Lomond the pair agreed to spend a few days there. Rather than pack up and set off, the athletic sister would spend two hours running and return. While the other simply relaxed, took in the view and prepared food.

We crossed paths regularly because they were parked close by, finally the vaneer sister revealed that her running sister was a world champion athlete – an iron woman. Suddenly the constant running made sense. She was keeping up her fitness. That evening we had a barbecue and quite an in-depth conversation about travel, vans, camping outdoors and wild camping. The running sister, Charlie, revealed that not only was she an iron woman, but a lecturer at one of England's top universities. She specialised in neurobiology and had a fixation of how the mind responds to endurance. Her behaviour made complete sense. She was essentially her own experiment. What made her increasingly fascinating was that she was fifty-five and one of the world's top female endurance athletes. She certainly had a level of focus that one could sense just by being in her presence. The other sister was completely different. She had married young and had four children. They went off to university which meant she was experiencing 'empty nest' syndrome. Her husband wanted her to find something she loved and that was her van – Alicia Van-stone.

CHAPTER 42

PADDLING, PLOPPING AND FLOPPING

I ended up extending my stay by one extra week plopping around and paddling. The thing is as much as I didn't want to go, the Isle of Skye was my next destination. I have found that I quite often rush journeys to get from here to there in the quickest most efficient way and time. There is the cliché: enjoy the journey, and prior to this trip I decided that I would focus on the ride. With no deadlines to meet – social engagements to get to, and the life treadmill filled with planning and organisation far away, the trip could involve flowing for once. Just go with the flow – erm how? That was part of the learning.

I left Loch Lomond at seven-thirty in the morning with Skye as the intended destination. That was the earliest I could depart because I was staying at a campsite that closed it gates at ten-thirty and re-opened them at seven-thirty. I was glad of that because it meant there were no cars or vans driving around in the middle of the night. However, when it came to an early start and getting ahead of the driving game, it wasn't so convenient. Admittedly I have a town/city mentality because the traffic in Bournemouth and surrounding area is nuts. To get ahead of the game you are often on the road around five-thirty to 'beat the traffic'. Well, in this case there wasn't a lot of traffic to beat, and that was a relief. The only thing that I would say is that there are huge lorries that travel at speed and can surprise you on a corner. What's more, the journey has a lot of bends and some very steep hills, so navigating them with a low gear is a must in some cases. Other than that, it was time to indulge in the journey.

The first part of the drive took me along Loch Lomond. That morning the sun cast a golden light over the pristine loch. There wasn't a ripple which made it appear like the perfect mirror to the sky. Since it was the end of May, the trees were flourishing and flowers were in bloom. The air carried a floral aroma and crisp leaf smells. It was a delight.

Blossom glided along. She seemed perfectly content taking the corners and the hills. 'Shit!' I jumped and swerved because the first huge lorry rounded a corner in the middle of the road. I was a tiddler in comparison and would not have stood a chance if I had not slammed on my brakes. The huge truck careered past. It carried petrol. If there been a collision it could have been quite an explosive spectacle.

I gathered my breath and decided to slow down for corners. I didn't want any more surprises and I was glad that I took that approach because beside the lake there would have been potential for at least five collisions with large trucks. Now, something that occurred to me was how lucky I was with the weather. It was sunny with no wind. I sensed that if it was windy and rainy that drive would have been treacherous. I am glad I had not thought about it beforehand because I think I might have frightened myself. Instead, I just got on with the adVANture.

One of the things that concerns me about big journeys is running out of petrol in remote areas. Admittedly, I am a member of a car assistance company; however, I try not to go below half a tank before filling up on big journeys. In my opinion it isn't worth the risk. I reached my half-a-tank buffer and pulled into a small village which had an automated pump. I paid with my card and filled up. I then parked, made a coffee and went for a stroll around and there they were… gnomes! Bloomin' gnomes again! It was as if I had a Scottish welcome gnome crowd to tell me I was on the right path. All around the area bug hotels and fairy doors adorned trees. It was so sweet. There were carved wooden pixie-like creatures and fairies dangling from any woody appendage. I sat and had a coffee and dark chocolate on a bench beside the fairies and gnomes. It seemed only fair to engage with them. I did sit smiling, it was so odd that I kept turning up at places with gnomes and fairies when I hadn't planned to visit the little creatures. Obviously I took photos and sent them to Teresa.

After drinking some water I began the journey through Glencoe. I have to say I was not prepared for how spectacular it was. Essentially there were cloud bands, crepuscular rays and blue sky. The mountain peaks reached up and were peppered with clusters of snow. In terms of enjoying the journey, I would stop at most of the view points and just take in the scenery. There was no rush and one could not help but indulge the feeling of awe. It was astounding how the weather kept changing which affected the views.

During that part of the journey I saw quite a few cars and only a few campervans, which surprised me. When it rained I would still stop, park up and open my side door. That way I could face out at the view. I would simply sit and take it all in. When I stopped at sunny locations I took a stroll. At some of the stopping points the mountains were beside rivers which reflected the sky. At other points rocks, that resembled sleeping giants clad with moss and micro-planets, were lit by rays of light. It was awe incredible. Plus taking the time to be completely present was an absolute delight.

After Glencoe I followed some small windy roads that took me through a loch area. Vast pine forests dotted the mountains and once again I paused, and had lunch, which I cooked in the van. All the while I relished the scenery. I realised I actually felt completely alive, awake and for once I was experiencing without fatigue. It had taken over a month for the tiredness to drain from the nervous system. I had not recognised how exhausted I was and how desperate my soul had been to take the journey. Yes, my unconscious had been shouting at me, but I had been avoiding it, caught up in the treadmill of life and attempting to remain 'safe' during chaotic times. Ridiculous really. In that moment I gazed over the loch and the forests - I decided I needed to listen to my intuition and that little voice more often. That moment was simply incredible and I was fully present within it. My heart thumped and I inhaled deeply. It was perfect.

I will be honest, I did take quite a lot of pictures of Blossom against the spectacular back drops. I felt so proud of her and how she was handling such a journey. The level of comfort and the joy of driving her long distances was something I had not anticipated. That in itself was a learning. She was perfect for my needs and relatively fuel efficient considering the terrain she was covering. I can't get over how I over-thought the journey when the reality was entirely different. I have to say I was concerned about that leg of the journey because it was a biggy at approximately five hours across mountainous terrain. I think it was one of the longest drives yet. In hindsight I noticed that I only get stressed when I rush… So to stop stress then don't rush. Simple!

I realised I was nearing Skye when I saw Eilean Donan Castle. Of course I had to stop and take pictures. The castle stands proudly on an island between Loch Duich and Loch Long. According to Google the Address is Dornie, Kyle of Lochalsh. When I first noticed the castle my heart skipped. The sun illuminated the distinctive turreted architecture and the blue sky made the loch a beautiful contrast. What a spectacle! I pulled into a nearby carpark and just sat once more, taking in the scenery. It was easy to imagine the old world of kilts and clans culminating at such an astounding location. There was an immense sense of history, beautiful architecture and power. Although, the thought of living there during a winter in the thirteenth century was less appealing.

After relaxing for a while, and taking a wander around the area, I realised I could have stayed in close proximity to the castle; however, my gut said 'Go to Skye'. I had always desired to visit and it was more important for me to reach that destination. I checked the map, Skye was just down the road. A deep sense of relief filled me. In fact Skye was just across Loch Alsh. I was nearly there and if I wanted to return to the castle then it was literally just a short drive. Admittedly I sensed that Skye would have more than enough to keep me occupied.

My heart pounded once more when I saw the bridge onto Skye. Since the age of eighteen, nearly thirty years ago, I have wanted to visit Skye. One of my college friend's mum's had retreated there. When she returned she was an entirely new and enlivened person. That transformation had stayed with me most of my life. So, Skye carried high expectations.

The bridge crossing was made slowly so that I could fully experience the views and the feelings of my arrival. The scenery from the bridge was vast and the height of the bridge was loftier than I had expected. As bridges go, this one was charming. What's more, It was easy to follow the signs to where I needed to camp. Within around twenty minutes I was on my site, set up and ready to luxuriate in a bit of relaxation. I set up, sat in my camping chair and that was when I met my first midge.

CHAPTER 43

SKYE, EDGES AND FACING FEARS

You know how you often hear about places and something about someone else's passion ignites you and makes you want to visit that same place in hope to have a similar experience. There are also those places that you stumble upon that are quite unplanned. Finally there are those places that you know exist and for the life of you, you can't find them. Well that all happened in one day on Skye.

It was probably about five in the morning when I woke up. First light must have been around four. I had forgotten that the further north you go the earlier first light is, as is last light. I think at that time of year – towards the end of May, the light only began to recede at around nine-thirty in the evening, which was my usual bed time. I know – talk about party animal! That is my bio-rhythm and on the other side of that I generally wake up around half-past five and am ready to rumble at around six (after black coffee and dark chocolate).

Well, that spectacular Skye morning began with a red glowing sun, a cool breeze and a temperature of a balmy fourteen degrees (according to my van 'outside temperature' gage). Admittedly, it did feel a bit nippy but that was no excuse to remain tucked up in the sleeping bag. Blossom and I were going to find the fairy pools before any touristy throngs got there. I had heard so much about them and wanted to get there before any kind of mass influx.

I set the Satnav to find the fairy pools and realised I was only around forty minutes away. What I had not expected was how fearsome some of the roads were. Many of them were narrow, others had edges and some were incredibly steep with some monstrous bends. I have a huge fear of edges and the thought of having to reverse backwards beside a steep edge to enable another car to pass was quite a motivation to go early. Ohhhh my goodness edges – when I think about edges they turn my stomach and make my innards flip. I literally hate them. Now I have made it clear that I HATE edges, we are of course about to go to the edge of edges. For the first part of the journey the roads were clear, but as with most of my empty road experiences, a huge HGV always seemed to thunder down a steep hill or round a corner in my direction. That morning followed the same pattern. I was on the inside lane, beside a steep bank when the HGV rounded the corner next to a steep edge. I slowed naturally and he continued without batting an eyelid. When I say he – the front of the Vehicle had BARRY written in large letters. I haven't met any women with beards called Barry to this date, so I assume the driver was a man unless it was a cleverly disguised woman – who knows?

Barry thundered past while I inhaled and allowed the adrenaline to pass through. A few moments later I turned left and followed a road down to the fairy pools carpark. There weren't any other cars parked, which was a delight. It meant that at seven in the morning I could luxuriate in fairy pool solitude. I quickly paid for the carpark and jogged down a path with a sign pointing to the fairy pools and in my haste I did not notice the exit route from the carpark because it would have ruined my fairy experience.

Now what I find amusing about the fairy pools is that I had a very different idea in my mind about what they were. I thought they were going to be limestone pools with really turquoise water – somewhat like the blue grotto in Sorrento or the limestone pools in Turkey. I was wrong. The fairy pools were a lovely series of pools with clear water that were supplied by a river and some waterfalls. I had seen pictures of people swimming in them. I considered a full body dunking but the outdoor temperature put me off because it was now around fifteen degrees. I popped my hand in a pool. Brrrr! As much as there is that whole movement of people jumping in cold water, my poonani/lady garden wilted at the thought of it. I did not fancy nippy nether regions for the sake of it. Instead I took a nice stroll, watched some rabbits and conversed with some sheep. When I say conversed – there is nothing like baaaing at a sheep that is baaaing at you. Luckily there were no humans to observe the intellectual exchange. The ewe found the grass very tasty, the water in the pools was very refreshing and yes sheep do get cold heads in the winter but they are used to it.

After such deep insights I thoughtfully continued my stroll, admired the surroundings and took photos of the scenery. It is funny how when you start to feel energised and in alignment with yourself that you can have a gut feeling that states it is time to move on. With that urge I returned to the carpark. On the way up the hill I noticed a series of steep edges – my worst nightmare! That was the exit route. I had no choice but to drive them.

Well, I took a lot of deep breaths and then guided Blossom along the hairpin bends. Oh my goodness – did I feel lightheaded and queasy as we rotated? YES! I took deep breaths all the way and placed absolute focus on driving. My van is wonderful and has a good turning circle; however, that did not alleviate the fear I felt every time it appeared as though I was close to an edge. I am not joking - I hated it. When I came to the end of the edgy–terror-ridden-terrain and joined the 'normal' road – I actually cried with relief. I then 'yeyed' my heart out to celebrate. Yeying is simply screaming yey!!!! At the top of your lungs. I know… Edges, heights and spiders are my absolute worst things. I went to the fairy pools and unintentionally faced a fear.

After that I decided that the next experience had to involve dinosaurs. So there is an area in Skye where a series of dinosaur footprints were discovered within some rocks beside the ocean. They were only visible at certain tide times, which happened to coincide with that current timing. I set the Satnav for the destination and… went round in circles for a little while. What's more, the roads were narrow with edges down towards that beach. This time I was on the outer 'edgy side' and prayed that no one drove towards me. I was lucky. Although once I parked I glanced up the hill and saw a huge mobile home on the edge with a very expensive car attempting to squeeze past the rocky cliff beside it. The mobile home driver appeared completely unphased, and then parked in a really inconvenient area.

I noticed a few people were aggravated by the mo-home positioning but decided to get on with the dinosaur hunt because it was nearing eight-thirty, which meant tourists were stirring and would no doubt descend upon the dinosaur destination. I followed the signs to the beach and began to scour the area for dinosaur footprints on the dark rocks. They weren't that obvious. I expected them to be large and very 'footy' but no... I kept finding rock pools and attempted to re-format the shape into a dinosaur footprint in my mind.

In the end I met a couple with two children who were also searching for the elusive footprints. We thought we would be efficient and broke up the area into quadrants, which we snaked around. There was a high pitched excited wail, 'I found it', screamed the six year old girl. The rest of her family and myself darted in her direction and there they were. There were a few footprints in an area. They were clearly footprints too. Each was filled with water where the tide had receded. We were all rather excited and wondered how large a dinosaur would have to be to make such a print considering how heavy it had to be to impress its foot into a rock. Admittedly we speculated about fat dinosaurs and then came to the conclusion that the print would have been impressed into a mud which must have fossilised. How very exciting!

After a bit of a chat about Skye, camping and edges, the family mentioned there were also fairy hills, not just pools. Well how could I resist? That was my next destination. I headed back to Blossom and glanced at the road I had arrived on. There were plenty of cars on the edge and there was no way I wanted to go that way again, so I took another road out which looked quieter and less edgy. I was right.

Shortly after I pulled in and set my Satnav to circumnavigate an area with castles. From there I would descend into the fairy hill region. Now this is where I mentioned that sometimes you cannot find what you are looking for. On that road I saw some monumental scenery and some astounding rock formations but the castle I expected was completely different. It was a set of ruins. I parked where the Satnav suggested and sauntered down the road to find what resembled a pile of stones. I had found the place but it was not what I was looking for. It was lovely enough but isn't it funny how you can have an image in your mind and when the location does not match you feel as though someone has misled you. It was me - I misled me with my expectations. That was a lesson in itself. I have to admit I was disappointed but I had seen dinosaur footprints and fairy pools all in one day. With that in mind I returned to Blossom and enjoyed the stunning drive, with empty roads, along the coast, around and down to the fairy hills. What's more, there was a fairy circle awaiting discovery. Fun!

I can honestly say the fairy circle and mounds were the highlight of my day. Dinosaur footprints were dumbfounding but the hill formations around the fairy circles was perplexing to say the least. The mounds were incredibly moundy and high. There were a couple of major mounds with plateaus on top. There seemed to be numerous people taking photos very close to steep edges. Some were too close and my legs turned to jelly (and I was not even up the hills).

I followed the path beside the mounds to the fairy rings where there was a stone in the centre and a number of rings circling out from the central stone. The sun came out and illuminated the area and made it feel lush, green and magical. What a wonderful accident to stumble upon because of a dinosaur footprint.

I pottered around there for a while, walked the hills and then had my lunch on top of a mound overlooking the scenery. I glanced up at the two main plateaus and watched tourists doing extremely risky selfies. My legs went to jelly again. I am always amazed by what people will do for selfies and often wonder about evolution of the human amoeboid. Whoever reads this will have to figure out what I am saying – although I call a mass of human idiots 'people soup' and a single entity that contributes to the human soup – a human amoeboid. So many people say they are not judgemental – well I am – I find it hilarious. I am astounded daily by the levels of wombattedness that people achieve. One of my favourite examples was when I worked as an expedition leader and took some people on a tour of the Falkland Islands. A group of passengers climbed over a fence saying 'Beware landmines' so they could get a photo of themselves on an area of landmines. Clever?

Oh and then there was the lady that wanted to get a picture of herself stroking a Komodo dragon on Komodo Island – that is after I informed the passengers that if they were bitten by one of the creatures then a bacteria/poison would be released into their blood and gradually rot them from inside. Well… she still wanted a picture with a 'cute dinosaur-like creature'. How such people live as long as they do is a mystery.

Anyway, I ate my lunch and headed back to Blossom. I had decided on a scenic drive back to the campsite because it was coming up to three in the afternoon. A somewhat late lunch. Back at the carpark I ended up chatting to some other vaneers. They had screens on their windows. I asked if they were there to combat the midges – they were.

'Have you seen any midges yet?' I asked.

'Nope… It has been too cold and too breezy but it is midge season. We are just prepared because we were here last year and were midge buffets.' They were clearly amused by the fact they had invented the midge buffet. I found that entertaining. Although when the midges were at full capacity it was more like a feast. After a tour of their van they pottered about, produced a number of midge deterring products and some head nets. I laughed at the head nets. 'Do you really wear those? You will look like a bank robber!'

'They might look ridiculous but they are worth it. Mark my words... When you accidentally stumble into a midge mist you will be glad that you have cover...' The woman then put the net on her head and fashioned it in a very glitzy manner. We all laughed. Their words resonated with me. I realised that I probably needed some form of midge protection. As soon as I saw a chemist I would invest. Although I was unsure about the head nets. I didn't want to be mistaken for a bank robber.

The drive back to the campsite was equally spectacular and involved numerous scenic photo breaks. The island was beautiful to say the least and the views were endlessly breath-taking. Skye was completely different to what I imagined, which seemed to be a common theme on my journey. However it surpassed my expectations. I literally fell in love with it, as well as falling in love with Scotland as a whole. I felt so blessed to have followed my desire to visit such an awe-inspiring place. All the while the midge conversation buzzed in the back of my brain. Talking of intuition, my gut made me feel I needed to invest in some proper midge murdering moisturiser. Unfortunately it would be a couple of days until I listened to that gut feeling and luckily I managed to purchase some repellent before the midgey onslaught.

CHAPTER 44

HEAD NET HILARITY

A couple wearing head nets walked past my van. I found it comical because they looked like they were wearing tightly woven fishnet stockings over their faces. I wondered whether my new neighbours were going to attend a 'weirdo in wondrous outfits' convention. Nope – they knew what was about to descend upon us. Apparently they had been studying the midge forecast on a midge location map.

What was interesting was the first few evenings on Skye there had been quite a breeze. Plus it was rather nippy. That evening the wind dropped, the sun shone and the temperature was a balmy seventeen degrees. Evening drew in and the sun cast golden light. It was definitely time for a meander amongst the magnificent scenery. Before I left the van I sprayed myself with a well-known midge repellent and coated myself in a specific oil moisturiser that is known to be effective against midges. Luckily I purchased the products that day after overhearing a conversation in a bakery about being prepared for the midge-fest.

Now, what was amusing was that I headed to the local chemist and was met by a rather forthright woman. I believe she would have been most excellent at tossing a caber in the Highland Games. She might have also been deft with a cannon ball on a string with the intention of taking down moving targets.

Rather than spend ages browsing, I went over to the counter and asked her what the best products for midges were. She smirked and rolled her eyes. She then directed me to an entire area dedicated to midge protection including face nets, candles, sprays and oils. I glanced over at her because I noticed her watching me.

'So what do the locals use?' I asked.

'WE don't…' she replied in a strong Scottish accent.

'Don't what?' I asked.

'We don't use anything…' She replied.

'So how do you deal with midges?'

'WE just get on with it…' She was matter of fact and peered at me like I was a 'weakling'.

'But you must get bitten…' I responded thoughtfully.

She shrugged and continued stacking the shelf beside her.

I thought I should approach with a slightly different tact. 'What do you recommend for tourists?'

'The whole lot,' she said without looking up.

By the way she wasn't being rude. It seemed that was her highest level of being friendly.

'What even the head nets?' I asked

'Particularly the head nets...' She said stacking some haemorrhoid cream.

I watched her to see if she was winding me up.

'You'll see,' she said, sitting back on her heels.

I didn't buy a head net. I wondered whether the locals might sell the ridiculous face-stockings to tourists for a joke. That would be the kind of thing that I would find hilarious. When we worked on cruise ships the new crew were sent with buckets to go and collect steam or mist. There were other little jokes like that played on new recruits and the face-net farce resembled that kind of wind-up.

In the end I returned to the counter with my selection.

'You made the right choice,' she said as she typed in the prices to her register.

She was right.

After taking a long trek along the breezy beach that evening I climbed into Blossom. The air became still - that meant trouble. I quickly packed away all of my stuff, and closed all the van windows (after I had made my dinner). I then ate and glanced out at the couple beside me. They could not tell I was watching them with a bemused look because my tinted windows concealed my head net stalking.

The couple wore full-on midge protection outfits while they attempted to sip glasses of wine in the romantic setting. The pair drank wine through face nets and gazed adoringly at each other as a mist of midges rose into view. It was insane. It was as if a huge wall of ash rose from nowhere. The area reminded me of old televisions where all the black and white dots moved around. Or imagine a dense dark dust being blown across a valley while you are standing in that valley. Or imagine a sand storm but replace the sand with midges. The midge mist was thick, buzzed, and had depth. The swarm landed on my neighbours' white table and turned it grey rather than black.

The couple continued to make the best of their evening with their midge defences. I will be honest, I didn't intend to leave Blossom. Thank goodness my porta potty was inside. I didn't want midges to feast on my behind or undercarriage in the act of pee-wee desperation. Luckily that night was my last night on the west of Scotland. I would never have believed that midges could create such thick clouds or cluster in such abundance. Ironically, after hearing all the midge horror stories on line and in the van social media groups, I thought that the midge-fest had been grossly over exaggerated. In that moment I realised how lucky I was that there had been strong winds and low temperatures when I arrived. I was grateful to experience Skye without the little nibbling midgey mouths. Had the conditions been different then I would have been a human feast or a buffet. Thank goodness!

I watched the head net lovelies do their best to enjoy the sunset and felt for them. I was somewhat impressed by them too because they were not going to be deterred by becoming human midge nibbles. They sipped their wine, gazed at each other adoringly (even with their noses somewhat squished by netting) and revelled in the midgey experience. After sunset the pair headed into their van, they had special coverings on their doors which meant they could sit inside and gaze out. That was odd because they could have had dinner head-net-less – maybe those head nets made them more attractive. I couldn't understand why they would sit amongst the mist when they could enjoy pretty much the same view without all the netted paraphernalia... Maybe that was part of the experience. Maybe head nets were their fetish – who knows?

Admittedly I was perplexed, but no one could know what was going through their minds. My mind stampeded with midgey stories and head net justifications. Maybe they had been sold the head nets so they intended to make the most of them... What I did know was that as much as I loved Skye, I was glad to be leaving the following morning and hoped that none of the midgey shytes snuck into Blossom. Luckily I was going to drive east where apparently there are less midges, or they arrive later in the year. I have to admit I now understood why so many people avoid parts of

Scotland during midge season. Witnessing a wall of mass midgey nibblers rise up is terrifying!

My final little learning/realisation was that I would never laugh at anyone wearing a head net again (I say that now) because after seeing such potential biting midge mayhem - the net protection was actually sensible. Would I choose to wear one myself? Erm, as much as I would like to say that I am a head net convert, I am not. I would rather avoid midge season all together and I probably won't laugh at the head net wearers because when I return to Scotland I will make sure that I am nowhere near midge season, midges or in a state of mind where I find head nets cool.

That morning I woke at six. I ate pre-made chia seed porridge with fruit, which meant I did not have to open any windows to cook. I then arranged my van for departure – all from the inside because the midge mist was vibrantly buzzing away. They were ready for any bare flesh. Before I left I had a wash in the van and noticed a few of the buggers had made an attempt at infiltrating my clothes. They had succeeded; however, the oil had coated them and their little bodies remained lifeless on the surface of my skin. I had become a midge slick. As much as it was disgusting, I would rather that than be feasted upon.

I put on a fresh set of clothes, did my checks and was glad I had packed up the previous evening. Rather than climb out of Blossom and do my checks, I drove her forwards and checked through the window. I then circumnavigated my pitch in the van to make sure I hadn't left anything behind. Thank goodness everything was inside because in truth I would have left any 'stuff' rather than brave the midges to retrieve it.

On the way through the campsite gate I breathed a sigh of relief. I literally had seen the rise of the midges at the beginning of midge season and my timing was immaculate as I made my way to Glenmore. It was going to be a spectacular journey with good weather... There was only one thing that was bothering me – the fact there were thousands of midges crawling all over my windscreen and lurking outside my windows. I needed to gain speed in hope they would be blown away!

CHAPTER 45

THE PERFECT PITCH

There are times in your life when you cannot believe your luck. That was one of those moments for me. I arrived at Glenmore and had a chat to the warden on the gate. She offered me two options on my electrical hook-up pitch. I could be in the main field (with lots of campers) or amongst the trees and in the midst of quiet. It is obvious where my choice would lead me… However, I had no idea what a wonderful choice I made. So, imagine this, being perfectly placed in a quiet spot, which was just two minutes away from the lake, amongst trees and far enough away from neighbours to not be bothered by any noise they make. In one direction I could see snow-capped mountains – which was a bit odd for June; however, they looked lovely.

After setting up, I inflated my paddle board and took a stroll down to the beach area beside Loch Morlich. I marvelled at the sight before me. Mountains, perfect reflections and a whole loch to explore. What made it all of the more delightful was that the loch was without hundreds of boarders, even though there was a place to hire kayaks, paddle boards and other 'marine craft'. Now that expression 'marine craft' makes me smile because it is obnoxious terminology. I am aware of that…

I was so pleased because the lake was large enough to explore and had a river flowing into it. I was soooo happy because I was there for five days and sometimes a person books a place for a chunk of time and thinks 'why?' In that particular case I thought 'thank goodness.' Oh and another aspect I really liked about the site was the fact that there was a shop and a bar there. It made it a pleasure to have food options, especially once you have set up and don't want to cook or have limited choice in the fridge.

That afternoon I had a lovely nap and then took to the water. The weather was calm and a balmy sixteen degrees. I am one of those people who is always cold, so marvelled at the locals in their swimwear and shorts. I couldn't have even thought of such a limited amount of clothes with snow lurking on nearby mountains.

As I paddled I felt my body settle into the rhythm and made my way to the centre of the loch to just sit and take in the view. It was stunning in all directions. The loch was so calm and the reflections of mountains, pine trees and the sky were pristine. The water was clear, there was quite a lot of 'weed' in the water; however, the colours were beautiful and it added to the experience. There were a few little 'nooks' to explore around the loch and there was a sense of expanded time. So much so I ended up being on the water for around three hours. I took pictures with my phone but almost fell off the board when I saw it was eight-thirty and I hadn't eaten yet. Woops! The thing is it was June and I was high up North, which meant that the sun set later and it was hard to gage the time. Plus when you are absorbed in something you love, time becomes irrelevant.

With a sense of reluctance, I paddled back to the van. I could have stayed on the water for hours; however, I realised I had prime opportunity to fly my drone. There weren't many people around, so I would not bother anyone and there was only a light breeze. I put my food on to cook and set up the drone. I have to be honest, I am still learning to fly the drone and... I am pretty crap at it. I took a few little films but the battery ran out pretty fast. I was happy with what I recorded but it came to a rapid end, which was a shame, although probably a good thing. I think it is apparent that when I get involved in creativity, paddling or walking I lose time and end up completely immersed in what I am doing. I can spend hours and then suddenly 'wake up' and realise that time has evaporated, I haven't eaten and have almost forgotten where I was.

After droning I headed back to Blossom, took out a cider and ate my dinner: baked veg with salmon and some peas. Simple, tasty and even better when gazing out at the view. I made a contented sigh because I could not believe my luck. I had the perfect pitch in my perfect location and... I met my neighbours who were absolutely lovely too. They were respectful, had a beautiful long-wheelbased van and lived thirty minutes down the road from where I lived. It was nuts: you travel from one end of the kingdom to the other and meet fellow travellers who set off from just down the road from where you live.

CHAPTER 46

PINE PARADISE

The sense of joy I felt when I woke up in Blossom and gazed out at a wild vista could not be measured. I was in a real state of bliss. Of course there were weather conditions, temperatures and other people that contributed to my experience. However, to lay in your van and watch sunrise over a super calm lake certainly ignited the soul. What's more, sleeping amongst the silent pine trees provided a depth of sleep that I never achieve at home. That is probably because I live close to a main road. Admittedly there is something in pine trees that promoted calm, and the smell of them instantly relaxed me. Of course there is also the freshness of the air.

That morning I gazed out of the window at the loch from inside my sleeping bag. I was extremely cosy, there was no one around and the temperature was probably around fourteen degrees. Not too hot or cold for a sleeping bag. I laid for a while and then made myself a coffee shot with my small 12V coffee machine and ate dark chocolate. There was no rush, I didn't have to be anywhere and I didn't have to do anything. I could go with the flow once more.

I sipped my coffee and made myself go slowly but I had 'that urge'. I wanted to be on the lake because it was like a mirror. The mountains were illuminated and the snow was a pinkish hue on the caps. It didn't take long to get on the water. I simply changed into shorts, and a wetsuit top with bikini beneath and headed for the shore.

After a short paddle I sat at the centre of the lake... the reflections were pristine. What was above was shown perfectly below. I felt so lucky and so pleased because there was no one else out there. For a moment I felt a pang of fear but if it all went wrong, I had had a lovely time up until that moment. In the end I just took in the scene: the mountains, the reflections and the glow of the sun with the lack of people. A sense of pure solitude filled my being and I was immensely calm. It is rare to feel like that so I savoured every moment and immersed myself in the feeling.

By eight in the morning I was ready for my proper breakfast and cooked salmon, eggs and veg on my grill. As I sat and ate I noticed a couple wandering by so said hello. They asked me how the paddle boarding was and then asked if they could see the layout of my van. It wasn't very tidy but I obliged anyway. It seemed they had been intrigued because Blossom is such a tiddler. I then took a stroll with them to their van and it was a beauty. They had hired it. It was a high top with a long-wheelbase, porthole windows at the back and a large bed which traversed the rear. They had a shower and a proper loo. It really was luxury in comparison to mine. Yet Blossom was easy to drive, manoeuvre and fitted into parking spaces. Every van has its virtues, I would guess that is why people are so curious about other people's lay outs and set ups. Could you imagine walking up to someone whose house you liked and ask for a tour? It would be funny but not considered acceptable. At the other end of the scale there is van life where most vaneers are a little bit nosey and ask to have a peek inside at any van-portunity.

The couple and I hung out for a while. We had coffee and cake. Again it was nice to just enjoy rather than have to be in a meeting or at a location. By eleven I was a bit 'bored' so I considered going for another paddle; however, I decided it was worth going for an explore of the area. The surrounding forest and mountains with the numerous footpaths were ideal. I ended up hiking by the river and circumnavigating the lake via a well-signposted path. I chatted to lots of random people, which I often find quite funny because I assume I will be alone, or try to be alone. On the walk I met a few couples, a number of backpackers and a few paddle boarders who were trying to paddle down the river. Everyone was cheerful and seemed glad to be alive. One naughty little pup took a liking to me. While I was sitting down by the river it climbed into my lap and stuck its tongue up my nose… Lovely! Especially after what it had been sniffing. Still, I do love dogs. I would love my own.

After my marvellous meander a nap was necessary. Later I tucked into some snacks before launching back onto the loch to paddle across in the other direction. I spent another couple of hours exploring. There were only another couple of boarders but they were paddling in the opposite direction. After about two hours I then realised I had forgotten to eat a proper meal and needed to head back. Funny how that happens. I made a simple meal of salad, chicken and veg. I took one of my seats to the beach and sat watching ducklings chase each other while gulls swooped on the loch. The sky turned an amazing shade of red and the air cooled. What a simple and lovely day. No big dramas, just a wonderful time in nature. I felt so blessed. Joy can come from the simplest experiences. I realised that I spent a great deal of time pursuing states of joy and bliss, instead of allowing them to unfold. It was simple: a van, in a forest, by a lake, with a paddle board, meeting nice people, having some cake and then eating a nice nutritious dinner in the evening accompanied by a sunset. It wasn't having lots of money, or being in a five star hotel. All of those ideals and I was happiest with simplicity, nature and the novelty of experience.

CHAPTER 47

ANCIENT WOODLAND AND LOGGING TRAILS

As much as I could have kept myself entertained for weeks by simply paddle boarding on Loch Morlich, I felt that I should at least trek around the surrounding area. With that in mind, I set out early one morning, after I had been paddle boarding, and circumnavigated the lake by foot. I then joined the logging trail, which took me through some beautiful forest, along by river Luneag and into Rothiemurchus forest. The trees were ancient, twisted and blooming lovely. There were plenty of pines too; however, the gnarly trees were most appealing because they had a feeling of character about them. They reminded me of the old fairy tales and how they might up their roots and walk away… Many had faces and shapes on them which were really quite rude-looking. That made them more appealing in my mind.

The trail provided plenty of vistas just to sit and take in views. Although something really jumped out at me: there used to be a husky sledging centre but it had closed down due to global warming. As I walked I processed the reality of that. The temperature had risen so significantly that snow did not stay around for long enough to warrant a husky sledging centre. The thing was, in the nearby areas there were ski runs and the site where I was staying hired out skis in the winter. It seemed there was still enough snow for that.

What struck me about the logging trail was the contrast between the 'order of pines' and the gnarl of the ancient trees. Both were beautiful in their own right. Both provided a sense of nature and peace. Yet it was quite apparent how we, as humans, attempted to order nature. Yet nature always re-ordered into random chaos in the end.

I continued my amble along the river and could feel a blister brewing, so took the opportunity to sit, have a coffee from my flask, a drink of water and an oatcake from the shop. It was tasty, not too sugary and provided the carb hit that I needed. I decided not to go too much further and felt the desire to turn back. I took a slightly different route back and discovered a huge tree. It definitely demanded a bit of a tree climb. Since no one was looking, I climbed up into the canopy and gazed out over the lakes and mountainous vista. I loved it. There I was sitting in a tree in Scotland gazing out at forests, mountains and lakes. What could be better? So I had another drink and the rest of my oat cakes. A picnic from a branch. How wonderful!

I sat for a while and watched numerous cyclists enjoying the logging path. No one noticed the random woman up in the tree, and that in itself was a pleasure. I was a stealth tree climber. I will be honest, I sat up there for a long time. Well as long as I could manage because I have a bony bum and it began to ache. I considered how wonderful the location was and how glad I was I had taken the trip. I had definitely fallen in love with Scotland, its people and the paddle boarding potential. I often wish such moments would last longer, but the reality was that I had at least two hours walking until I would reach Blossom.

On the way back I walked the beach area of Lake Morlich and met some lovely dogs who were having the best time darting in and out of the water. There were a few paddle boarding pups as well who were sitting at the front of their paddle boards taking it all in. What a life!

By four o'clock I was back at Blossom and definitely needed a nap. I realised I had walked for around six hours and could feel a potential ache developing. To counteract the ache I did a quick yin yoga session for the legs and then retreated into my bed and passed out. I woke up at six-thirty in the evening and considered eating. Realistically that was not an option because the lake looked magnificent. I grabbed a couple of cans of fizzy apple juice from the fridge, some water and some stuffed vine leaves. I put them in my 'paddle pack' and headed out onto the loch. There I sat gazing at the spectacular reflections.

Every time I sat at the centre of the loch I marvelled. The cloud formations were epic and the mountains, with their snow caps, sent me into states of wonderment. There was pure peace out there and no people at that time… just me, the board and nature. I loved life… Physicality was a blessing and to be able to perceive such phenomenon ignited my soul. I spent about half an hour focused on deep breath work, paddled and then rested again. I was back at Blossom by around eight-thirty. I realised I hadn't eaten properly again so cooked some veg, some salmon and added an egg. I sat on my fold-out chair considering what an amazing day I had experienced again. It was so simple, yet throughout I had been present. I had not had to do anything or tick a task off a list. That was happiness in itself.

CHAPTER 48

THE KELPIES

After close to a week up at Glenmore it was time to move on. I was reluctant to make a departure and considered extending the stay. I checked the calendar on my phone and realised that I had passed my 'time tipping point' and was on my way home. That meant time would speed up and I should move on to the next part of the adVANture. I had decided that the trip from Glenmore to Northumberland was quite a biggy and decided to break it up by visiting The Kelpies, two metallic lattice horse-head sculptures that reached thirty meters into the air. They were located between Falkirk and Grangemouth, beside the new extension to the Forth and Clyde Canal. The sculptor, Andy Scott, completed the beauties in 2013. The Helix, a parkland project, was created to connect the local communities, all sixteen of them. It was a fantastic idea – one I was drawn to visit.

The Kelpie, according to legend, was a shape-shifting spirit that lived in the Scottish lochs. It looked like a horse. Plus it may have retained its hooves when it took on human form. Well, with all of that in mind, and the fact I read about the details of The Kelpies after the visit, I don't think that anything could have prepared me for the excitement I felt when The Kelpies first came into view.

To see the mighty, marvellous metallic structures rising from the earth took my breath away. So much so my stomach flipped. The moment I caught sight of them was when I was at the pinnacle of a large hill and trying to figure out, using the Satnav, where on earth The Kelpies were. The location was not logical at all because they were on the edge of a built-up estate and beside an industrial estate. Although, actually it was logical because that area probably needed regeneration, investment and beautifying. Those Kelpies certainly beautified it. Imagine seeing two giant horse's heads rising up out of the earth, set amongst a series of canals. What made it such a monumental sight was that the silver horse structures were set against blue sky.

Now you will have to forgive me because I am quite naïve in terms of the Scottish infrastructure and I had no idea that there was such an elaborate canal system – I only discovered the history once I had visited. I wish I had researched the trip a little more thoroughly rather than just winging it. Well it wasn't winging it exactly, more of a quickly compiled plan made around large volumes of work and long hours. The last thing you want to do after spending ten hours a day staring at three screens is stare at another one when you can be outside in nature.

Back to the canal system – marvellous, and what a way to navigate Scotland – via houseboat. I literally had no clue that was possible. I followed the Satnav directions, unfortunately I don't really have a huge amount of faith in Satnavs and always have a back-up paper map. The amount of times I have ended up in random fields in the backside of nowhere! At times it was funny, but at other times, when I was a photographer, and photographing a sports event, turning up at a random barn in a field two miles from the event became tedious.

Another time I ended up in a really dodgy estate when I was supposed to be meeting someone at a country pub. It was the kind of place where you locked your doors and did not leave the car. Needless to say, when I was being directed through a less than pleasant built-up area towards The Kelpies, I wondered whether history was repeating itself and the universe was testing out its favourite stunts. Talking of favourite stunts, on that journey I had two near-misses when it came to joining a motorway and a multiple lane transition close to Edinburgh.

On the whole of the journey around England and Scotland I had three very dangerous moments. The first was Spaghetti Junction where I picked the wrong lane, a huge roundabout on the edge of Glasgow, and joining a motorway at an area beside Edinburgh. All three situations were terrifying and I can tell you when I saw the sign for The Kelpies I certainly felt a huge sense of relief. It meant I could stop and that I had completed most of the big drives.

Now, the next little 'I could be lost moment' was because as I descended into the 'valley', I could not see The Kelpies from the road. According to the Satnav there were quite a few roundabouts which appeared as though you would be reversing back on yourself. Never mind, I decided to stick with it and see where I ended up. A few moments later I emerged from the estate, navigated a couple of roundabouts and found myself at a very well run visitor's carpark. Luckily I was there early, which meant that the throngs had not yet arrived. Now I say that in jest; however, coaches turned up later and there was a human onslaught like ants over a ripe apple. With that in mind, an early arrival is a must or a late evening arrival for the night time Kelpie illumination. That was another sight that takes one's breath away.

I will be honest, I could have spent most of the day there pottering around. There were some nice cafés, a little shop and plenty of trails to walk along. In reflection I felt as though I attended a Scottish travel buffet and had tasted many of the possibilities. However, in the future I would like to return, take my time and have more of a gourmet meal of Scotland. I said that because that was my last Scottish stop before heading across the border into Northumberland. Another beautiful area; however, I did feel a pang of sadness because crossing the border back into England meant that I was on my way home. Yes it is a nice feeling; although, there is that tipping point within travel - the first part feels like it's taking its time. Then there is a sudden shift and the travel momentum gathers - you feel as though you are the stone rolling down the hill. Time speeds up and you are suddenly transported back to 'normal life'. When that happens it is worth noting it really is about savouring every place, focusing on the enjoyment and being present in the now.

CHAPTER 49

NORTHUMBERLAND EXPANSES

Alarm bells sounded in the back of my mind when a man approached wearing an apron with a busty bikini-clad figure emblazoned upon it. In addition, that same chap strode with urgency wielding a two-pronged-fork with a half-cooked sausage impaled upon it. I had just arrived and set up Blossom when this chap essentially jumped out from behind his motorhome with an urgent look upon his face. My first instinct was that I had done something wrong… But the contorted grimace was actually his welcoming smile. 'Hello neighbour,' he called in the 'I am your new best friend tone'.

Shit!

My gut said 'Fuck off!'

Bearing in mind I requested a 'grand-sized' pitch so that I could park in the centre and be able to maintain 'boundaries'. Well that did not work because suddenly there was an impaled sausage being waved at me urgently. Admittedly, I had given up my plan for the luxury of anti-sociality. Diving into hedges was taking its toll and wearing full camouflage was not an option. So I made my best attempt at not appearing pissed off and waited for the sausage-wielding, apron-wearing camping neighbour to provide an insight into what on earth he was up to.

'Ahhh you have just arrived. I can see you are setting up. Are you alone?' All of that was said in one urgent breath.

'Yes.'

'Isn't that a tiny van? Do you sleep in there? Do you have a tent? Why else would you need such a large space? We are all friendly here… I take it you are a member of the 'club',' he said. The impaled sausage waving was relatively distracting. I still thought 'Fuck off!'

'Errr…'

'Is this your first time? Have you got plans? Do you want a sausage? They are the best around… Venison…' he said before I could get a word in.

'Erm I have just driven for five hours and need to chill out and get my bearings. It is very kind of you to offer me a sausage; however, I already have food prepared that will go off. Otherwise that would have been lovely…'

I noticed his eyes glance sideways as a couple parked their motorhome. That motorhome was a similar kind to his, whereas mine was a tiddler. He seemed fascinated that I had a small campervan but quickly lost interest because across the way he had seen a 'new friends' couple.

Wielding his venison sausage he studied me, 'I get the impression you need to get yourself sorted… I will give you some space.' With that he turned on his heel and headed in the direction of the new arrivals. He was on a direct course through the campsite. What was interesting was watching how the other vaneers reacted to him. Some literally stepped out of their vans and reversed back in. Others appeared to leg it to the loo, as if taken by a sudden onset of food poisoning. A few pretended they were asleep and others turned the other way. A couple of dogs even hid under the vans.

I glanced around; those who were not in his sight appeared from their vans, peered around the side and checked the 'coast was clear'. A few smiled at me as if I was some kind of survivor.

After erecting my privacy tent, where I can use my own shower and loo, I headed over to the shower block. I have mentioned before when I use the facilities on site I store stinky shoes and things like my outdoor grill in there. It enables a bit of a clear out and space in the van. On the way back from the shower block I passed the most unique retro campervan. It was a real beauty: there was bunting, a beautiful swirly design and plenty of daisies against the orange background. The couple sat outside reading and grinning.

'Hello,' they called.

I paused and went over because I needed to have a peek inside their van. 'Are you okay for a visitor?'

They nodded, 'Not all visitors though.'

I studied them.

'You were so lucky this afternoon. Mister Campsite Menace was on your case and you averted him. Well done,' the female vaneer said in a tone of complete respect.

'Campsite menace?' I replied.

'Yes, the chap in the apron. Once he has you he will just keep talking at you. He wants to make friends and invite you over. He uses the apron as a conversation technique,' she explained.

'Ahhh.'

'He came over to us and basically spent two hours in monologue. Jenny here went for a nap, came back and he was still telling me about his collection of fishing lines and tackle. I read my book to try and stop him but unfortunately he continued nonetheless. When I got up to go into the van, he attempted to follow,' explained the chap.

Across the campsite we noticed a flurry of motion and dashing. The campsite menace was on the rampage. He was red in the face and on a direct route back to his van. The couple and I rotated around the van in such a way that children hide behind trees when they play hide and seek.

'I wonder what he is upset about…' I said aloud.

'Someone has obstructed his view,' said Gill. 'Watch….'

With that the pronged fork was waved aggressively as the menace gave the 'view blocker' what for.

'What is it with people? Isn't it obvious I selected this pitch for the view and there you are thinking you can just turn up and block it! How dare you!' he waved his sausage fork like he wanted to begin fencing.

The view blocking fellow looked bemused. The rest of the campsite peered from every nook and hiding cranny they had used to avoid him. The situation was about to get nasty.

Well, the commotion rose, as did the voices. The sausage sword waved in an aggressive way by a man wearing an apron with a bikini-clad woman decoration was enough of a threat to force the view blocker to move on. Now, that was quite a sentence! The campsite menace was right to call the view blocker on his behaviour; however, his behaviour then re-evidenced the need to avoid him for the fellow campers. What made it worse was the menace was parked within my periphery. That meant I had to be clever in my movements. The campsite was fully booked. I was there for five days, which meant I had to be tactical. What's more I intended to spend most of my days visiting places or driving to nooks and hidden crannies.

CHAPTER 50

ALNWICK

At seven in the morning I discovered Patricia hidden between a recycle bin and a general waste container. I had just emerged from a nearby hedge because we were both avoiding the menace who was early morning ambushing.

'Found you!' I said, making her jump and scream.

'Is the coast clear?' She whispered.

'He's on the other side of the site. I can make him out by one of the new arrivals,' I replied.

'Phew... That was close,' she said standing up and brushing herself down.

We both laughed and kept our eyes trained on the distant menacing shape.

'Where are you pitched?' I asked.

She gestured at a plush mobile home positioned opposite me, which meant she and her husband were 'prime bothering real estate,' for the menace.

'Lovely van,' I said. 'Are you managing to spend much time in it?' I asked

She shook her head. We are going out as much as possible to avoid Derek.

'Who's Dereck?' I asked.

The bloke in the apron she replied.

Ahhhh. I had no clue of his name, instead everyone I had talked to had referred to him as the campsite menace. How funny.

'So have you been anywhere nice?'

'We were at Alnwick today. It is gorgeous. We come here every year and visit the grounds on each trip.'

'What is it?' I asked.

'It is an ornamental garden with beautiful ornamental grounds and a phenomenal fountain. If you have the day spare then spend the whole day there. I highly recommend it. You have to book a ticket though.'

I had nothing planned for the day.

'Shit! He's coming!' Patricia cried.

With that we both darted in different directions. Well that was it. I looked up the Alnwick Gardens and booked a ticket just like that. I ate my breakfast in the back of the van and then made my way to the lovely location.

From the moment I parked up I felt a sense that I was visiting somewhere very special. I entered through the main gate. On the way in, there was a fun wooden house that reminded me of a witches' tree house with all its wooden 'scales'. It turned out to be a restaurant, one that I would visit later.

I checked in at the reception area and turned to be met by a huge terraced waterfall in full view of a café terrace. The curves of the fountain snaked down to a large pool and the cascading water trickled over numerous shelves from the top of the fountain to that large pool. On either side there were domed hedges with small doors that led to a path. I had arrived early, so there weren't many people around. Of course I could not help but photograph. What made the images more impressive was the blue sky with perfect fluffy white clouds. All around the gardens were topiary hedges. I have a thing for well-cut foliage. It is probably influenced by my Japanese trip. The thing is there is a real skill to making a shape out of a hedge.

Now what made this place all the more fascinating was there was a poison garden. It had numerous poisonous plants and stories of infamous murderers who used the plants in potions to kill people or seek revenge. The black metal gate to the garden had the words 'THE POISON GARDEN' emblazoned upon it along with two sets of skull and crossbones. Beside the entrance there was a small wooden hut with a grass-covered roof. I have to say it was quite an insightful garden. Reading the stories of the rogues who had become infamous for using different plants to assassinate their intended targets was certainly enlightening. I spent a while studying the plants and enjoying the stories. It provided numerous ideas for assassin stories.

From there I went for a wander and stumbled upon a cherry orchard with numerous swings. There were swing terraces amongst the trees. Flowers bloomed in all directions, white cow parsley decorated the surroundings. It was magical! Talk about appeal to the inner child. So of course I went and swung.

From the swing I watched numerous visitors stumble upon the orchard. What I found intriguing was how adults responded to the swings. Many were reluctant to have a play. Instead numerous potential swingers glanced around, as if seeking permission to simply enjoy the sensation of being on an adult sized swing amongst a cherry tree orchard. Something about the 'seeking approval/permission to play' as an adult resonated with me. Why do adults have to be 'grown up?' That thought followed me around the gardens like a helium balloon. I spent over an hour just swinging, watching and contemplating. I had snacks and drinks with me, so could be in masticatory motion (I find that word combination amusing!)

After the cherry orchard swinging indulgence, I noticed another garden filled with water features and a huge variety of flowers. There were benches dotted all around to enable plant pleasure and floral fun. Numerous wooden lattices had vines and creeping plants interwoven onto them. There were some truly beautiful and unique flowers to view. I could understand why Patricia suggested a whole day there. Although I was also curious about the village of Alnwick. What enabled my curiosity to be quenched was that my ticket enabled me to leave and return on the same day. Since it was lunch time, I thought I would explore the village and return for the afternoon.

The village itself was quaint, with old style architecture. There were the usual shops and plenty of cafes. It seemed that the village was being used for a film location, as was the castle, so unfortunately there was security in all directions because some of Hollywood's renowned actors were apparently in the vicinity.

Since there were so many media vans, cranes and other film making paraphernalia, I circumnavigated the village and returned to the peace of the fountains and gardens. What I loved were the plant covered lattices that covered the pathways. Those and the large dome hedges with doors. There is something wonderful about standing inside a dome hedge with two doorways. It isn't often one can make such a confession.

With only a couple of hours until the gardens closed I decided to return to the cherry orchard and swing, gaze at trees and watch the clouds. Time flew by and I glanced at my phone. There was only half an hour until the place closed. What a shame because the gardens had been a delight. Finding Patricia squatting between refuse bins had been a lucky and fortuitous event. Maybe I should be thankful to the campsite menace.

Talking of campsite menace, when I returned, the site had a completely different vibe. People were sitting out on their fold-out chairs appearing happy. Some people lounged in hammocks and everyone seemed relaxed. Not one person was standing flat against a wall, crouching behind a bin or hiding behind a tree trunk. Well it turned out the menace and his wife had gone for dinner with some friends at a nearby village. Now what made me smirk was that the mobile home owners had gathered and allocated 'watch duty'. Each was doing half an hour by the main gate. When they saw his car they would sound a klaxon. At ten-thirty I was inside

Blossom preparing to go to bed when the Klaxon sounded. I glanced out of the window and there was a flurry of activity across the site. People folded chairs urgently or simply legged it to their vans and closed the doors. The menace, who was completely unaware of the response, drove steadily to his mobile home, climbed out of his car and stretched. He glanced around the campsite and said to his wife, 'Everyone goes to bed so early.' Little did he know…?

CHAPTER 51

LINDISFARNE

My brother always wanted to visit the Holy Island called Lindisfarne, just off the coast of Northumberland near Buckton and Ross. Now what was interesting about the location was there was only access to the island according to the tides. Essentially the road to the island was covered by sea water until the tide retracts. There was a short timeframe where you could cross, and a short window of time to visit the island because once the tide reached a certain level then there was no chance of returning to the main land.

There was a sign that stated 'DANGER! Do not proceed!' when the water reached the causeway. Apparently numerous visitors attempted crossing even though there was an incoming tide. Some ended up 'awash' and stranded when they were caught by the rising water. If a person got stuck then there was a ladder leading to a small hut where one could wait out the tide. The big question was would your car start after such a watery deluge?

It seemed that the tide could reach a height of four meters in depth. At the shallower end of the tide scale it could be one point five meters. I also learned that it costs around four thousand pounds for a helicopter to rescue those who are stranded. That is quite a costly mis-adventure!

As with most of the trip, and I am embarrassed by this, I found out about the places I visited while I was there.

Admittedly, I had heard about Lindisfarne. My brother had talked about it and when I was creating a route, it seemed an obvious break in the trip from Scotland to the Midlands. Yes, I know – that's what happens to someone who's time poor and doing a random 'Stuff it!' I learned my lesson there, and in the future, will definitely do a bit more research. Although, sometimes being spontaneous has luckily worked out – unless a person forgot to research tide times.

The conversations with locals or fellow vaneers have provided the most insight. In addition, prior to the trip I spent quite a bit of time on a social media group dedicated purely to women who had campervans. Their advice and insight was invaluable and non-judgemental. By making searches on the site there were quite a lot of recommendations for locations to visit and places to stay. When I searched out campsites in Northumberland, the one I stayed at was highly recommended. Numerous single women campers had stayed there and pointed out that it was a central location with good access to key sites. They were right.

Now back to Lindisfarne... The tides were perfect to traverse the causeway at seven in the morning. That was ideal for me because of that early morning biorhythm. It would take around thirty minutes from the campsite to arrive at the causeway. That morning was astounding too. The morning light, the countryside and empty roads made the journey to the causeway wonderful.

What I found on the way over was that I had no concept of how the causeway would look. What's more, I had never driven on a causeway. My mind went into overdrive: imagine if I had the timings wrong. All that kind of thing passes through an over-thinker's mind and that mind had not been focused on problem solving for months. It definitely had freed up capacity for mental churn and raising random fears like 'What if there is a tidal wave? How long did I have to get across the causeway? What happened if I broke down on the causeway and there was no one around? How far could I swim to get to land?'

Early morning, too much coffee and dark chocolate combined with an overactive imagination definitely provided some rather random mental incidents to solve. Well, I arrived at the causeway and double-checked the times. There were no other cars around. In fact there was no one around. There was a combination of bliss due to the quiet and fear. I could see the island and felt that it was probably about a five minute drive across. Rather than fear the journey I switched myself into a different mental state and intended to enjoy the journey.

Of course I had to take a few pictures because causeway driving was such a rare experience. I think what bemused me most about the causeway was it was a road with dark sandy/muddy flats either side. I didn't know what I was expecting but that road looked as though it was cutting through a dark sandy beach. I thought there might be a huge dip, but there was more of a gradient down onto the causeway. It is odd how we construct mental illusions, scenarios and images in our minds, only to discover that we are completely wrong.

The drive across the causeway was smooth, my mind provided a vision of a random great wave gathering momentum just as I reached the middle of the crossing. Of course that didn't happen; however, another thing I find fascinating about the mind is how it often creates worst-case scenarios and escalates them to the extremes. At one point in my working life I used to build risk generators to come up with the worst case scenarios on the stock exchange. I often wondered whether the years spent coming up with very extreme or random situations to apply to stocks had an effect on me. As an example a landslide in Peru, in a certain location, could affect the whole world's copper price. That copper price would then affect electronics, which could then increase the prices of technological items. It really was a worst case scenario snowball, and yes it was fascinating, however the mind became primed for holistic repercussions on a huge scale. So, with that in mind, there I am in the middle of the causeway considering the potential of a giant tidal wave and what I would do if I saw one in the distance. React, drive very fast and hope I would outrun it. Although the thought process made me think about thinking. Which was very much a snake eating its own tail.

As you may have guessed, I arrived safely on Lindisfarne Island, with no random tidal waves to outrun. I followed the Satnav to the suggested carpark, which was walking distance of the abbey and castle. I am pleased to say there was only one other van and one car parked in the carpark. The tourist droves hadn't arrived yet. When I glanced at the time I saw it was just after seven in the morning, which explained a lot; however, I only had time restriction. The tidal hours meant I had to look around and get back onto the causeway in adequate time. So, the tide time I chose was 6.40am and it was safe to cross back until 12.30pm, otherwise I would have to spend the whole day and could cross from 6.50pm until 1.00am in the morning. As you can imagine it would be easy to get stranded there. I would have been fine because I could have slept in the van, even if there was no overnight camping in the carpark. The thing is necessity would have removed the choice and no one would know I was in the van.

While I strolled over to the castle I wondered how many people got stranded on the Holy Island. I then had to stop and take in where I was. It was so easy to go through the 'visit a tourist destination' motions and speed visit the place. I paused and glanced around. The vast 'flats' that contained the causeway, spanned as far as the eye could see. Something I had found fascinating about Northumberland was 'the great expanse'. There was so much space and not many people. While I was driving I would pull in and just look at how vast the place was. There was so vast at times it felt overwhelming, like you were just a speck on a huge landscape. Well, you were essentially a gnat hovering in limitlessness.

The castle path was obvious because the castle stood on a raised mound and ran parallel to the mud flats. The area was rugged with fields dotted with sheep who were definitely trying to harmonise their baaaing. The sky was blue, it was breezy but warm with a lovely sense of calm in the atmosphere. There was an aroma of sea with a hint of seaweed.

On the way I saw a few people walking their dogs and no one else making their way to the castle, which opened from ten until five. That was probably why. I will be honest, I wasn't so worried about visiting the interior. Instead, I was more curious about the 'feeling' of such a place. I tell you what, the atmosphere really lifted the spirits and I sensed the expansiveness would send most visitors into the depths of contemplation. I can imagine how the stunning sunrises, sunsets and storms set against the raw surroundings would certainly evoke higher thought and contemplation. That, being away from humanity, and having time without distraction would enable personal insight, wisdom and revelation.

With all of that circling through my brain, it was most necessary to just sit on a bench and take in the view. Taking that journey had provided such a contrast to the speed of my usual life. As much as there was limited tidal time, I didn't feel as though I was in a rush for once. If I did miss the tide, I could potter around until six-ish anyway. It wasn't a problem.

I have to say I like stone walls. I don't mean general walls, instead I mean the ones that create borders to fields. Isn't it nuts that there are so many stones and… how much time people must spend constructing those walls? The thing is it wasn't just one or two walls, or for a short distance. Instead they went on for miles, in all directions. At a point in time someone had an idea/vision to create the walls. They had to source the stones, decide where to place them and how high to make the wall. All the while lichen prepared to get involved in the construction too. I wonder how many people look at a stone wall and think 'That is actually marvellous'. I do. My fascination with stone walls and how people create physical boundaries isn't something I often share in conversation. Instead, I admired how many stones had been piled on top of each other and arranged over such distances when so few people noticed or considered the implications of their making. On top of that, I loved how nature creeps in and plants weave into the walls with lichen and moss decoration. Those habitats are simply taken for granted yet, walls emerge from someone's mind because they need to create boundaries. I wonder what sheep make of the walls. The reason I mentioned that is because there were sheep on the other side of the wall I was admiring. They chewed grass and regarded me with blank expressions.

After appreciating the walls, I noticed the path that ascended to the castle. It was a stone path that was arranged like cobbles. That too was quite a phenomenon because all of the stones had to be transported and set down. The width of the path had to be considered in addition to the route. What I found interesting was cobbled/stone paths that don't run in straight lines. Instead this one meandered. It took a course towards the castle and then turned back on itself. It was clearly intended to enable a gradual gradient. I reckoned it was because carts needed to transport the different alcohols brewed there. That route was stunning too because red flowers decorated the area beside the path, before the water's edge. They weren't poppies, but were a similar colour. All the while clouds took on some rather amazing shapes and had smooth edges. The aroma in the air was filled with red-flowered pollen, grass, salt and sheep shit. A random combination, and one that made me smirk when I attempted to describe it.

Finally I arrived at the castle and gazed up at the rampart. It wasn't terribly large, but was very solid. There were shepherds' huts beside the path and very stony ground all around. The cloud patterns were phenomenal and all was silent. I stood in stillness, in quiet and allowed my mind to be quiet, another rare phenomenon. No one was around. Fantastic! I found a nice bench, settled down and opened my thermos flask to some very dark coffee which was accompanied by dark chocolate. Every sense was satisfied and a feeling of peace rose from my toes to my brain (that might have been the coffee/chocolate combination). I found it interesting that the feeling rose rather than started at the top and trickled down. In that moment I felt peaceful, satisfied and blessed. The Holy Island had done its thing and brought me into a state of stillness and connection. I loved it.

It's a shame that experiences come to an end. On my stroll back I wandered by the abbey and down a road where I heard some odd sounds. It sounded like wailing combined with grunting and aural squelching (I might just love that word combination). I met some people with binoculars who were stood beside a hill peering through their binos onto the beach. I paused beside them.

'What's that sound?' I asked.

'Seals,' they replied and handed me the binoculars.

I looked through at a mass of silvery dark bodies basking in the sun, on the shore. For a while there was still and then there was another seal ruckus. I handed back the binoculars and had a chat. It turned out the couple were staying on the island for the week and just indulging in being away. They loved wildlife and all of the flora and fauna. I did wonder whether they would get bored but without even asking they mentioned they were really enjoying not doing much and hoped to reach a state of boredom. They didn't intend to leave the island for the duration and would explore Northumberland for a couple of weeks after their 'retreat'. Talking of retreat, I became aware that the tide was going to turn soon and I had to make my way back.

I followed the road into the town, popped into a bakery and strolled around a gift shop. The island centre was filling up. My guess was tourists were arriving for the day. Well, I splurged on a new journal and some locally made brews and returned to Blossom. The carpark was already three-quarters full and I laughed to myself because there was a sign that said 'NO BUSKING Allowed on Holy Island Development Trust land'. It was random and had definitely put off any busking hopefuls. I checked the time and still had an hour and a half. On the way back I took my time on the causeway, photographed Blossom on location and enjoyed gazing out at the 'flats'. I marvelled at the volume of opportune cars and tourist buses traversing the causeway to the island during the last tidal moments. The Holy Island would be filled to brimming point!

When I arrived back at the campsite, I checked the area for the campsite menace. The coast was clear, so I indulged in sitting and writing up the experience. Later that afternoon I napped and then took a stroll along nearby footpaths. I saw buzzards and hawks hovering in the evening light. It was so calming to observe nature and its instincts.

CHAPTER 52

KIPPER LOVE?

I have to admit Northumberland was a complete surprise and a truly hidden gem. The more I think about it the more I realise now how Northumberland was a revelation. I had no idea it would be so impressive plus it carried a feeling of great expanse. When one strolled along the beach near Bamburgh, you felt like a lone ant stepping into a space so large that it was incomprehensible. On that particular day Bamburgh Castle dominated my view. It resided on the edge of some lovely sand dunes beside that limitless beach. The castle itself was teaming with myths and history. I found out that Bamburgh is behind some of the inspirations of Sir Lancelot's fictitious castle known as the Joyous Garde. When I delved into the history I discovered that the Bamburgh beast, an intricate gold form had been found there along with a rare patterned welded sword. The more I delved into the location the more I realised there was so much history. I couldn't get over it. In regards to the castle, the main transformation was taken on by William Armstrong who restored the castle. What's more, it still belongs to the Armstrong family. I found that out on Wikipedia.

While exploring the area I noticed numerous film crews setting up cranes holding complex cameras. All the while actors and actresses strolled around in historic costumes and bonnets. The thing is, as much as it was easy to get caught up in the filming glitz, there is more to Bamburgh than castles and huge beach expanses: there is actually kipper love. Who would have thought?

I was coming to the end of the stay when I had a chat with one of my neighbours. He was a nice chap and was spending a month on site. It was one of his favourite camping locations. Anyway during the chat he mentioned that the area was well-known for kippers, they were a local delicacy. I did screw up my face and think 'Yeh right'. However, I was on a proper adVANture and when I used to work on ships we would say 'If you can't identify it then eat it…' yep. That sounds ridiculous but there were grubs, ant-head paste and some rather odd looking creatures that were consumed in South Korea.

The fellow vaneer mentioned he had fallen in love with the Craster kippers and could not get enough of them. Kipper love? When I left him, the question 'Could you fall in love with a kipper?' popped into my mind. Well it is possible, especially when you get to taste one of the most delicious kippers known to Northumberland. With that in mind, and my adventurous spirit raging, a kipper seemed tame in comparison to some of the food I had consumed around the world. I had to give a kipper a go.

Well my first kipper in a bap experience took place just along the beach from Bamburgh Castle. After my first visit I remembered there was a hut with the word 'Kippers' on it, so I returned. I had frowned the first time I passed and thought 'What a strange little hut'. This time I made a bee-line for that hut with a smiley chap making kipper buns. Well, why not? So I did, and I have to be honest – the combination of butter, soft bread and the tastiest kipper one could imagine was a delight for the tongue to behold. I am not joking, even though there were bones. I savoured every tasty moment of it. I was really impressed. What made the experience increasingly enjoyable was sitting on a bench in the shade overlooking the cricket green and castle. Glorious!

Later that afternoon, when I advised my fellow vaneer that I had taken his kippering advice, he shook his head – 'You have to have a Craster kipper!' Craster was fifteen minutes away. Two kippers in one day? No! That was just extravagant. The next day was free and I wanted to clear my kipper-acious palette overnight. I wondered what was so special about the Craster kipper and soon discovered that it was down to the oak smoking of the kippers that took place at the central smoke house. The oak smoking turned the kippers a golden colour and created a flavour that was divine. What's more, the village was filled with kipper 'hunters'. It seemed that Craster was at peak kipper season and the smell of oak smoked kippers didn't put anyone off. Instead the smoky fish aroma could have actually been attracting tourists from miles around – like wasps to jam.

That evening I informed my neighbours of the Craster Kipper experience. They were pleased for me and then informed me that the campsite menace, in his bikini-clad image of a female on his apron, had been on the rampage around the site. He had decided to corner numerous vaneers and demanded to see the layout of their vans. I noticed him trudging across the field wielding tongs and dived into Blossom. He had no idea I was inside due to the dark tinted glass. Luckily his mobile home was positioned on the side away from my door. That meant I could sneak back and forth without detection. I have to confess I watched him and his wife sitting beside their van. He talked and talked and her eyes kept rolling back in her head. She was clearly bored and had no escape. It was intriguing to watch the dynamic. At some point she must have fallen in love with him or thought he was her ideal man. A weird thought!

Well I thought I had a natural 'menace detector' but unfortunately one can be caught off-guard. That night the menace cornered me, I was coming out of the showers and he said 'It is good to know that you are showering…' He hooked me in.

'Some of the other campers were confused by your behaviour. You are parked by the showers and loos yet you have a dual privacy tent set up. We wondered whether you were OCD. A few of the other campers decided you must have OCD to have more than one privacy tent,' he spouted like some psychological expert.

Hmmm. I do find it amazing how complete strangers generate stories about a person. He then informed me that they had decided I was single due to having OCD and that I was definitely travelling to get over it. Gosh what a yarn! I let him talk and realised there would never be a gap for me to respond, not that I intended to enter 'the game'. I wasn't going to let him know my privacy tents held all my excess stuff from the van and one had my paddle board inside. I certainly wasn't going to justify my behaviour to a stranger wielding an impaled sausage on a fork. So to end the conversation I said, 'You'll have to excuse me… It is difficult having heavy periods while camping. One doesn't want to make a mess.' I waited, watched his expression contort and then smiled to myself as I headed towards Blossom. Strangely he didn't bother me again.

The lovely couple I had met driving the orange retro split-screen noticed the conversation and waved me over once the menace had departed. They were curious about the conversation. They had never seen the menace scurry away from anyone. I explained what I had said. They gazed at me in admiration.

'Genius!' they both muttered. They then went on to tell me how the menace had ingratiated himself for nearly two hours the previous day and had talked and talked at them. He had forced his political views down their throats. In the end, after attempting to politely excuse themselves, they both got up to go for a nap in the van. He tried to follow. When they said they were going for a nap he asked to look at the interior layout. They said no that they needed a nap and he actually threw a tantrum. In the end Mark, the chap, said to the campsite menace that they were going to take a nap and would prefer it if he gave them some space. He did not take the hint, so the pair climbed in the van, closed the door and closed the curtains. The menace shouted 'How rude…'

Later on, when the couple woke up, he came over to apologise and invited them over for drinks. The pair refused and that evening went out to dinner to avoid him. Luckily two new vans parked in close proximity to the menace, and he met his like – another chap with a barbecue apron of a sheep. The pair became best buddies and barbecued together. Multiple menaces could work as team. It all turned out well in the end.

After all of that, I was feeling a little smug, but something must have been in the stars because that evening there had been a drop of rain which had created a few muddy puddles. Now I do have a word of advice: Never drop your knickers in a muddy puddle and stroll across a campsite with a smile/grimace on your face.
It was an accident but not that kind of accident. Instead, an innocent visit to a shower block unfolded into an unsuspecting embarrassment. Since England is renowned for inclement weather, why would anyone be surprised when a beautifully sunny day quickly transformed into a torrential downpour combined with forty mile an hour winds? I had waited in my van for a gap in the clouds and legged it to the shower cubicle. The delight of hot water flowing with power to actually remove soap suds from the body and shampoo from one's hair can be compared to the first time a person

eats chocolate after abstaining for a month. Ohhhh what a joy!

Wearing fresh knickers and clean clothes, I gathered up my showery belongings and headed across the site. The divine comics (in charge of the weather) precisely coordinated the wind to pick up. At the same time the rain wall charged towards me. I was wearing flip-flops and realised I had to leg it... sooo did precisely that. Running on water-logged ground is not something I would advise, especially across mud, rather than around it. My natural instinct was to take a direct route based on the physics of the speed of the wall of rain and the distance to Blossom. A couple of skids across the mud later, and while I was off-balance I threw my pyjamas and knickers in the air. The pyjamas came off unscathed but the knickers splashed down in a particularly muddularily gloomy puddle. Without a thought I grabbed them and grimaced as I launched back into a flip-flop running manoeuvre and skidded once more. This one was more slipping down a mud slide because there was a slope involved. Anyway, in an attempt to maintain my balance I waved my arms, releasing my muddy knickers rapidly into the air. They were then diverted by a huge gust of wind onto the screen of a luxury mobile home.

FFS!
My flip-flop floundering slide came to an end when my bottom touched down. The rain beat down and I was soaked. With a sigh, I pulled myself together and glanced over at the mobile home. Could I get my

knickers back without detection or did I need to abandon them completely? I then had the image of people knocking on vans to determine the owner of the soiled knickers 'dumped' on the luxury mobile home owner's screen.

Stealthily removing muddy knickers from someone's windscreen is tricky. What made it worse was there was a muddy knicker shaped impression left behind. Should I knock on the door and apologise? How do you explain such a sequence of events? It was beyond me. Had anyone seen? Could I escape with my muddy knickers un-detected? Was there CCTV? All the while it pelted down. The muddy knicker impression would be washed away. I took a deep breath, darted back to Blossom and placed the muddy knickers in the wash bag. I then changed my sodden clothes.

I glanced out of my tinted windows to see the luxury van owners, wearing their wet weather gear, pause by the van and glance at the windscreen. The muddy knicker impression remained. The couple appeared confused but not too bothered. One pointed at my long flip-flop induced skid mark and muddy bum imprint beside the van. Had they figured out the sequence of events? They used their windscreen wipers to smear the knicker mud across the screen. I felt bad because they were forced to face my unintentional skid mark. I could have apologised but instead I wrote my apology down: *If you are the owner of a beautiful luxury mobile home with the shape of muddy knickers splattered across on your windscreen – it was me. I am really sorry and hope the event did not ruin your stay. I am sure you will understand why I didn't come over and tell you what had happened. Kind regards...*

It was an accident and my advice to anyone is never drop your knickers in a muddy puddle, particularly on a windy day. Luckily the above incident happened on my last evening and in the morning I left early and made my way to Buxton.

CHAPTER 53

BUXTON

Things did not go smoothly because I received an email from the spa hotel I booked stating that my stay had been cancelled. Admittedly I was somewhat surprised by the last minute cancellation which was sent at midnight the night before I arrived. I only read it that morning when I stopped to get petrol. Talk about peeved. I was really looking forward to luxuriating in a spa.

The thing was the email made no sense. In essence the email stated that my stay had been cancelled due to the fact they were only allowing NHS workers to stay there. I wondered whether there was a glitch in the system from Covid. I attempted to call the hotel but I kept being re-directed. Well I tried multiple times to make contact and could not get through. I took the hint from the universe and scoured the camping app for a site near Buxton. In the end I visited one of the female van forums and found a highly recommended site. It was a fifteen minute walk from Buxton and on a bus route – perfect. By seven-forty-five in the morning I had booked three nights and made my way there as soon as I had filled up with petrol. It was a long journey and a spectacular one. I had intended to deviate to the Angel of the North but there had been a huge accident on the motorway which slowed the traffic. I decided I just wanted to get to the site, set up and chill out. I then intended to go to the spa and find out what had taken place.

When I arrived at the campsite I grinned. The area was green and the pitch I selected was perfect. It was beside a well topiaried hedge and the nearest tent was quite a way away. I couldn't hear anyone else and noticed that once I had set up the nearest tent arranged their stuff so others were deterred to join us.

My set up meant that I did not have to look at anyone, tents or vans/cars. It was perfect. I ate lunch, considered a nap but was irked by the spa hotel. Since it was only twenty minutes' walk to the spa I thought I would make a visit to discover what had happened.

Well I have to say Buxton is beautiful. The architecture, the parks and the gardens are wonderful. I took a gradual stroll into the centre, followed the map to the spa hotel and stood before it. Numerous people sat on the veranda wearing white bathrobes. They definitely were not purely people working for the NHS unless they had adopted spa robes as uniforms.

Oh I forgot to mention, I dressed well for this little visit. I mentioned before about my spa attire. I had intended to go to a spa in Buxton and Bath to round off my trip with luxury. Of course that was thwarted by the email. Anyway I went to reception and asked about the cancellation of my booking the previous night. The receptionist did her best to justify what had happened. However she was talking shit so I asked to talk to the manager and showed her the email. She was shocked and very apologetic. I had not been charged for the stay but I have to say I was really aggravated because I had been looking forward to luxuriating.

In the end we talked to the I.T department, who realised I had booked the spa during at an I.T upgrade. Somehow that had linked my booking to a Covid email and at midnight the night before my stay it had randomly sent that email cancellation. Weirder things have happened to some of the systems I have worked on, so I accepted that explanation. However, when I asked what could be done the duty manager said there was nothing they could do because they were now fully booked. She did not offer any recompense. I have to admit I was seething. I took a few deep breaths and decided I did not want a bunch of idiots and sequence of events to ruin my trip. So I studied them all, imagined a huge elephant turd descending upon them and felt better. Weird how that makes a person feel relief. I then understood why people sought revenge. I spent the rest of the afternoon exploring Buxton and enjoying every moment. Later during that stay I sensed that maybe the universe had sent me to the campsite to meet a particular couple to hear their story.

Once I have set up on site I generally like to leave Blossom on site and take local transport to visit nearby areas. That is, if there is local transport and I am not in the back of beyond. On that occasion I was staying at a lovely site just outside Buxton and decided that it would be rather wonderful to walk to the local bus stop and head over to Bakewell to sample the pudding and the slice. What I charming little journey it was.

The buses were at regular intervals, so I took one from the market square and enjoyed being driven. The thing with driving is you are always navigating roads and attempting to find places to park. By taking the local transport you can really take in the scenery and travel through local villages on bus routes, rather than go the most direct route. I rather like seeing some of the quaint villages that I would not have considered driving through. Admittedly, travelling by local bus takes time and there are lots of stops on route. I was not in a rush. Instead, I could immerse myself in the journey and cherished every moment.

I have to say the vistas from Buxton to Bakewell were epic, especially as it was June and everything was in bloom. All of the villages were vibrant with flourishing gardens and an atmosphere of cream teas. It really was a delight to see how people live in such remote little villages.

Now, I have heard a lot about Bakewell and upon first impressions I was not disappointed. The village, as busy as it was with tourists, was gorgeous. Beautiful cottages, flowers, a river and plenty of benches to take in the scenery. There was also a pretty park area.

As I walked along the banks of the River Wye, I noticed a bridge with an abundance of locks – love locks. This bridge has been a site of love declaration for years and has over 10,000 love locks declaring love for couples and families from all over the world. Imagine a bridge of love! LOVE IT! I did wonder how the love locks situation began and it seemed that the locks began to appear on the weir bridge in 2012. There was no specific trigger event, instead one love lock appeared and then another and another. How wonderful that there is a physical demonstration of love in the world. Especially after what the world has experienced in recent history. Anyway... After such inspiration I felt it was definitely time to have a Bakewell tart in Bakewell. However, what I didn't expect was that Bakewell pudding was actually what I should have been tasting.

I stumbled upon a quaint café located up a flight of stairs and found a nice seat looking out of the window. I studied the menu and decided on Bakewell tart, although, the pudding was also listed. Well, the proprietor came over and I asked a very simple question. 'I am in Bakewell and notice there is tart and pudding. Which should I have?'

He smiled and said, 'The Bakewell pudding is what Bakewell is famous for.'

After a bit of a conundrum and an argument with myself I found the best solution and decided on both. Yep! It was 'fatty Friday,' and I felt it wasn't worth going all of the way and not experiencing all Bakewell had to offer. My goodness I was glad I did. I will be honest, I went for the traditional tart first with coffee and it was very tasty. It was a pastry with an almond cake-ish layer, jam and icing. Definitely sugar-head-rush-tastic. I definitely felt satisfied in the cake consumption realm; however, the Bakewell pudding was a whole new pudding-game – it was delicious! It was served with custard, and / or cream. It was a proper pudding! It had a jam roly-poly or a spotted dick pudding consistency about it. It reminded me of winter, visiting grandparents and a sense of cosiness. I cannot recommend it more. Not only had I been inspired by love on the bridge, I had just ingested the equivalent of dessert ecstasy in the form of Bakewell pudding. What a wonder! I literally couldn't have wished for a better experience.

I admit that after both the tart and the pudding as my lunch, I had a sugar high. It seemed appropriate to take another constitutional around Bakewell to 'walk it off'. I admired the gardens and then went and sat in the park beside the river. Once I had digested, I headed back to the bus stop to enjoy a gentle journey back to the edge of Buxton before strolling back to my campsite. Of course I indulged in an afternoon nap in the van. Who wouldn't?

CHAPTER 54

DEATHLY DESTINIES

When I woke up I noticed two children hiding in the hedge close by. They were watching me. They seemed fascinated by Blossom and my set up. They were part of the family camping on the other side of me. They were far enough away to not bother me. It was just a little odd how these two young boys were both sitting in a hedge watching my every move... I would discover that their story was pretty harrowing.

After another full day tour of Buxton and indulging in ice cream in the park, I returned to Blossom for my evening dinner. The lady beside me went and pulled one of the boys from the hedge nearby because he was watching me again. Anyway Debbie, the lady, informed me that the children weren't her's instead they were her partner's. She said the boys were both a bit odd. They had been adopted and after two years of finally being part of a family her partner's wife was diagnosed with cancer. She then departed the world within six months. The children both developed abandonment issues and extreme behaviours. Debbie and her partner met in the hospice because her husband and his wife were in the final throws of life at the same time. What do you say to that?

Well, life decided they were going to fall in love because both were in grief when they ran into each other at a local coffee shop. The pair discussed how they were dealing with things and said they would support each other. They were both so authentic, helpless and vulnerable that they fell in love. They sat with each other's pain and were there to support and comfort each other during the grieving process. The thing was Debbie understood that to be with Ralf she had to accept the children. She was honest, 'The pair of them piss me off! But the lives they have had are horrific. You can't help but feel sympathy for them. It does not justify their behaviour but it makes you understand why they do what they do.'

We chatted some more and Ralf passed by. He had just ordered pizza and the family were going to sit and eat together. She glanced at me and said, 'It all puts everything in perspective.'

She was right and I realised that I could have been luxuriating in a spa or I could have heard a story of two very real people falling in love through the strangest of circumstances.

My last day was spent not doing much, tidying up the van and preparing to go to Bath. I was going to a luxury hotel and spa. Nothing was going to stop me. Anything that I no longer needed was going to be thrown away and my camping clothes were going to be kept separate from my spa clothes. It was when I studied my spa attire I realised I was lacking some nice shoes. So I popped back into Buxton and purchased some smart trousers, with some rather lovely shoes and a couple of nice tops.

I threw out a couple of old t-shirts and some worn-out walking trousers to offset the purchase.

That evening I had the pitch to myself because the couple beside me had left with their two boys. I did find their story fascinating. It was such a pre-ordained set of events to bring two people together. Debbie had said she had felt as though it was destiny and that on the other side her husband had got together with Ralf's wife and made them meet up. I found that a lovely thought… They had phantom vetters and ghostly matchmakers.

With the evening light casting long shadows, I sat back in my camping chair and gazed at the lime trees. There was a gentle breeze and those willow-the-wisp seeds (that look like fairies) floated through the air. I only had a couple of days left before I returned to real life… The trip had gone so fast, had been so enjoyable and had been filled with stories from wonderful people. I knew I was lucky and blessed. I just wondered how I felt about returning to normality, the social treadmill and routine.

CHAPTER 55

BATH

Okay so I admit it, after all of the stays in Blossom, a spa hotel for a couple of days made me incredibly excited. It was my intention to treat myself. I followed the Satnav into Bath and it seemed to take me all over the place. I was sure I knew where the spa was but followed the voice on the phone. Yep we were lost, or experiencing areas of Bath that I had no clue existed. In the end I pulled over, pulled out the map and drove to the location of the spa, which was precisely where I thought it was. What I didn't know at the time was the Satnav had taken me through a 'clean air zone'. Apparently you have to pay for the pleasure to drive through clean air. I had no clue such a system existed and you only know what you know, and you can't know what you don't know. So, I only found out when I was fined over one hundred pounds for driving through the 'clean air' district. Luckily I only found out about the fine a week after my return otherwise it would have ruined my stay.

Eventually I arrived at the hotel for two nights of luxury. I arrived at four and checked in to a wonderful room with a giant and comfortable bed. I called reception and booked in to the pool and spa area. I quickly changed into my swimming costume and headed to the pool. Oh my goodness, to be able to swim, sauna and hydro-pool! Bliss.

I swam for an hour and then calmed the swimming when a woman with a child on a giant inflatable speed boat dominated the pool. I had completed my swim but wanted to watch the reaction of the other swimmers. It was hilarious. Everyone tutted but no one said a word. Instead the child and the mother dominated the pool with the inflatable.

I took my leave, returned to the room and had a bath. Yes a bath in Bath. It is amazing how wonderfully luxurious it feels to have a bath after close to three months using a 12V shower or a shower block. Feeling refreshed and clean I made my way to the main restaurant and ate a tasty, posh three course meal. Scallops, followed by chicken breast and a toffee pudding. I almost cried with delight. Having food cooked for you is wonderful, yet when it tastes like bliss in food form then that ups the ante. At that point I felt a bit guilty because my trip was focused on camping and vanning, which had then ended in a spa. Did that make me fickle in the world of adVANture? I certainly wasn't being a purist. Maybe I should have camped, but really... Nahhh! Sometimes one needs to get perspective and the spa was my excuse. I had had a lovely time in Blossom and deserved to celebrate.

I lasted until nine o'clock that evening. I was satisfied and tired. I made my way back to my room, put on my new pyjama set and passed out until nine in the morning. I slept that long without a pee! I ordered breakfast to the room and gazed out of the window onto the grounds. They were pristine, decorative and filled with ancient trees. I could have happily spent the day gazing out at the ornate grounds filled with water features and sculptures. However, I thought I should at least venture into Bath.

I am so glad I did because there was a photoshoot of a cat in a pram with the Bath's Royal Crescent in the background. You know when you say something aloud but thought you said it in your head. Well I cried 'WTF!' Just as a chap with his spaniel passed by.

 'I thought the same,' he said.

We stood in mutual support as the cat was arranged in different attire and positions in front of the well-known architecture. The owner was both unphased and determined in her approach to the shoot. The cat attempted to resist but it was futile. I have to say it isn't often you witness a cat in a bonnet and a Victorian styled dress one moment transformed into a Viking with a helmet, plats and a bit of armour the next. It was random and fascinating.

The dog walker and I went our separate ways after about half an hour because it was apparent the cat photographer could be there all day adorning her cat with all manner of wacky outfits.

I made my way into the centre, took a walk by the canal and visited some galleries. Bath has a wonderful atmosphere which was highlighted by the fact I wandered down a street covered in colourful bunting and flags. At the end of the street was a telephone box decorated with fake grass and flowers. It was a novelty and one I would remember.

By two o'clock I decided to return to the hotel through the park. It was around twenty eight degrees and too hot for me. I took a wrong turn based on the Satnav and found myself scaling a hill to an epic view of Bath. It really was awe inspiring. I had never been to that view point before and stumbled upon it by accident. Beside the view point there were allotments filled with all kinds of plants, wind chimes and oddities. Of course there was an arrangement of gnomes. I could not have finished my trip without a bunch of gnomes making themselves known.

After detouring through numerous streets, I studied the layout of the area and the map on my phone. I found a route back beside the canal. Okay, I admit this, I had no idea there was a canal system and that you could travel to Bristol on it. My meander along the canal provided huge insight. There were numerous canal boats going slowly and enjoying the journey. Each narrow boat had a different name and some even had dogs on the bow.

I found a nice seat and watched one narrow boat navigate a lock. The Captain came over and had a chat. It turned out that he had also navigated the canals in Scotland and spent at least a month each year on a narrow boat. He then advised me he had friends who had sold up and purchased narrow boat homes. Didn't that sound familiar? Boateers rather than vaneers.

I sat for a while and met two other narrow boat crew. One set were brilliant at manoeuvring while the other crashed into the wall. I did laugh and so did they. They said they hadn't been drinking.

The last part of my walk took me through the park. What a lovely park it was too. There were numerous joggers and plenty of people sitting in the shade with a picnic. That was it... That was a moment where I witnessed life in a space and time. It reminded me of the impressionist paintings of the Victorians sitting picnicking in parks.

When I returned to the spa I went for a swim. This time there were no giant inflatables and I did not chat to anyone because I had filled my chatting quota. Although I was fascinated by a well formed woman wearing a gold swimming costume. She was the shape of a glamour model and strutted around with a glamorous atmosphere. I did not see her enter the water, but she did make sure that she arranged herself in seductive poses on the loungers beside the pool. I realised her bosoms would make good floatation devices and wondered whether they would allow her to do a decent front crawl. Maybe she would have to revert to breast stroke. Who knew?

That evening I opted for dinner in my room because I wanted something quick as I decided I wanted to sit out on the grounds until sunset. There were little dells to explore and some beautiful fountains to sit beside. I luxuriated in it all accompanied by a Rhubarb and Ginger fizzy drink. I spent the evening absorbing the ambience. Once the sun set I saw bats and noticed there was a golden full moon, a super moon. That was my last night of my adVANture. In the morning I would return home. Could the trip have been any better? Who knows? The thing is I sat there and my body was relaxed, I knew who I was, what I was capable of, and that life had provided me with the most wonderful opportunity. I felt blessed, alive and grateful all at once.

As it was my bed time I stayed up later, had a bath and went to bed. To my surprise I woke up at nine-thirty in the morning. I ate my breakfast, took another wander around the grounds and marvelled at topiary. I was reluctant to go home but it was time. A new life with a new me awaited. It was just a case of driving a couple of hours to get home.

CHAPTER 56

RETURN TO REALITY

After three months living in Blossom, where one has to tidy, re-tidy and tidy again, the thought of being at home and making a mess then going to a different room actually appealed. Stepping out from my usual life was lovely and having all that experience was phenomenal. Yet, returning home provided a sense of stability. When I stepped into my flat I realised I had accumulated a lot of 'stuff'. I needed to say 'Stuff it!' to stuff. What is funny is how when you are away from your stuff, you don't think about it. So why accumulate it. Returning home with fresh eyes resulted in a huge clear out. The less stuff you have the less you have to clean and the less mental 'stuff' burden you live with. The more you clear out the more potential freedom you have. That is just my opinion. I thought I was pretty minimalist after living from a suitcase on cruise ships for years. Yet returning to my flat I was surprised to notice that I had amassed quite a lot that I did not need.

During my time away I realised my brain needs a challenge, puzzle solving and a comparison. Could I live a life in a van the whole time? I guess that comes down to having to or not. If one had to then they would adapt. The thing is what I love is routine, structure and problem solving. Having the time away made me enjoy my freedom. Being in a spontaneous state and not really having any problems to solve (other than finding routes to and from places) was a completely new experience. Admittedly, being lost doesn't matter when you have a van and you can sleep anywhere. Everywhere has exploratory potential. That in itself is a joy.

Upon reflection, is there much that I would have done differently? The answer is no – the trip itself was perfect. The thing I learned about myself was I always tried to fit too much into a day. There were some days when I should have just slept and rested. Instead my natural curiosity and desire to experience resulted in me making the most of every moment and pretty much filling every space. My 'fit-it-all-in' mentality dominated the journey. That is wonderful, but I needed to rest and take it slow. I also realised that a hammock enables proper stillness and contemplation. Who doesn't need a free-standing hammock to lounge around in under the awning?

Another realisation was that in my mind I had thought that I would find solitude. The fact was that no matter where I went there were people, even in remote forests. The world is very full and there wasn't as much space as I expected. This came down to the dream versus the reality.

I think it is a shame that my heating did not work when it was needed; however, I am very glad that I invested in a sleeping bag that keeps one warm up to minus twenty degrees. I am also pleased I had a lighter sleeping bag should the weather have been warmer. It never reached a point when I didn't use the minus twenty sleeping bag.

I discovered hot water bottles are saviours. Two is definitely better than one. If I was going to advise a newbie to vanning of anything I would say – good socks, head torch, hot water bottles and a decent memory foam cover. Invest in a really good sleeping bag if you don't have proper heating in your van.

Don't sleep naked, not that I did; however, there were some rather awkward nude-cidents.

We are rubbish - now what spending long periods of time in a van does, especially when you go off-grid, is reveal how much waste we generate. I am just one person, yet I could create a bag of rubbish each day. It was astounding and a concern because I had not realised how bad my individual rubbish generation was.

Always take a paper map because Satnavs have taken me to ridiculous places and the battery on my phone has conked out at crucial navigational moments. If I had not had a paper map then I would have been in some serious travel trouble.

In terms of time duration: I think I might have added an extra night to each place. I had not considered that the travel day was essentially a 'no' day. Every new location required time setting up and taking down. Of course you can always leave your bed down. I learned there was no point rushing because when you decamp in a rush it makes the new set up slower. It is worth packing away well so when you arrive at the next location it is easy and efficient to set up. Whichever way you approach setting up and packing down, the time will add up to a similar amount. My solution for the pack up and pack down issue is stay longer and visit less places. Alternatively visit as many places but travel for longer. There is always a reason to stay longer – if you like a place. Quite often a person can extend if they haven't pre-booked their next site.

Also when one arrives they have to get their bearings. Again, there is no point rushing. In the future I will factor in additional time and allow more time to go with the flow and find out from the locals what is worth visiting.

On the trip I noticed some common themes. One of them is how we respond to situations. We all enter a set of events, yet we all respond in different ways. The weather up at the Lake District revealed that lesson.

Finding balance in my life is something I find tricky. I often have to completely throw in the towel and scream 'Stuff it!' I then have to find a reason to go and do what I want to do. It is as if I have to justify my decision to friends, family and strangers. I am done with that now.

Another common theme was that there were a lot of people preparing to depart the planet. When they realised they had limited time they made the most of the now. This made me question how we live our best lives now, rather than wait for an unguaranteed future. The answer for me was little and often. Make sure that regular fun trips are factored into life. Little, lovely, local and often. These little trips will hopefully stop me reaching complete fatigue.

CHAPTER 57

THE PEOPLE WE MEET

One of the female wardens, at one of the places I stayed, said to me what makes the trip is the people we meet. I think that is some of what makes the trip, and I have to say that sometimes it can be the people we meet who ruin the trip too. However, that time I was lucky. Everyone I met was friendly, had quite a story to tell or a number of stories to share. Most of the vaneers I met had plenty of van life experience. There were a few who had hired vans to make sure it was what they wanted and two of them decided that hiring would be the way forwards for them because the type of van they liked would cost them around sixty to seventy thousand pounds. They felt that if they purchased one outright then they would not get their money's worth. They would rather hire on a bi-annual basis and know they didn't have the hassle of parking, maintenance, insurance or general concern for the vehicle. It made sense really.

Another thing I found was how you started to recognise vans, styles of vans and then run into the same people in different places all over the country. I ran into people on opposite sides of Scotland, which wasn't that surprising but when I ran into them in the New Forest, well that was a bit of a shocker. I wonder whether certain people have a particular taste in location or pitches and then gravitate to places of a similar set up.

As I said I was lucky in who I crossed paths with. Everyone was accommodating, invited me for drinks or barbecues and were generally jovial, had stories or had plenty of great places to recommend. The trip was wonderful and some of the stories from couples and how they met was inspirational. It was as if they couldn't not meet – a proper destiny. Yet, what I found peculiar was how few single men and women I met on the epic trip. I often wonder whether couples invite me for drinks and food because they are concerned that I am alone. Alternatively, maybe they fancied a fun new playmate to chat to. Whatever it was, the people I met were amazing: the couple who danced in the rain and made the most of everything, the two ladies who enjoyed hanging their large knickers on trees to dry, the couple who met in the hospice when they were looking after their respective partners, plus all of the lovely people who recommended places. I even appreciate the campsite menace because his presence enabled me to meet some wonderful people. Finally the chap who revealed the fact that there was a tick on a dick on the site. Amazing or what? How often do you hear that? Not often but then when I shared the story I met three more chaps that had ticks on their dicks. I was astounded – what are the chances a trip-tick-on-dick episode. The tick on the dick story is in another 'Stuff it!' book – *VANDERLUST*.

Anyway, the reason I set off on the journey was to have silence, serenity and solitude. The funny thing was I found community, connection and stories. Talk about the other end of the scale - yet wonderful. Maybe what we think we are searching for is the opposite of what is seeking us out.

CHAPTER 58

SMALL WORLD

There are times when synchronicity blows you away. The likelihood of something happening or people crossing paths is so remote that it seems clearly destined to happen. This happened a couple of weeks after my return from my big trip. I was already having adVANture withdrawal symptoms, so I booked a pitch at one of my favourite sites in the forest. I had just finished setting up and a couple wondered over and said 'Hello Ruby'. The chap patted my van and said 'Hello Blossom.' I studied the pair and couldn't place them. I knew their names but still could not place them. The pair smirked and asked how long I had been back. I said a couple of weeks. They had been back three weeks. So I must have met them on the trip somewhere. I asked where they were set up and they pointed to the far side of the site. They told me that they had been coming to that site for years and both had had grandparents who had taken them camping there, so they had lovely memories.

I had to get some water, so I suggested I walk with them. I then saw their van and realised how I knew them. I had met them up in Glenmore. They had stayed beside the lake, just along the way from me and were originally from Southampton. They were a lovely couple and their van was absolutely gorgeous. It had portholes at the back. Those portholes had made an impression on me because I had spent so many years at sea, working on ships and had peered through portholes daily, particularly when we were arriving in port. Seeing the portholes had made me consider that style of van in the future.

As we walked the couple updated me on their trip. They had gone in a different direction when we left Glenmore. I had gone to Northumberland and around the coast whereas they had chosen to go down the middle of the country. They had had a wonderful time and gave me a list of places to stay, should I make a similar route in the future. Of course we were astounded because of the likelihood of meeting each other in a remote area of Scotland and then meeting a couple of weeks after our trip in the local area was rare. The world is small, synchronicity is great and like gravitates to like.

That evening, after I had set up, I went over for drinks with them. They asked how well my solitude seeking had gone. I laughed a very hearty laugh and said I gave up. I didn't stand a chance. I mentioned that the only solitude I managed was in the middle of a lake. Everywhere else people would gravitate towards me and me to them. We found that amusing and then spent the evening filling each other in on all of the random events from our trips… They loved the campsite menace they had seen a naked woman locked out of her van and a nudist in the night accompanied by an owl orchestra.

CHAPTER 59

THE BIG QUESTION...

Oh and finally the big question that people ask me. What happened to Ryan – did he get done? As with so many of these cases, many of the women he was ripping off were having affairs or felt stupid and ashamed they had lent the chap money. When the investigators contacted eight out of the nine ladies listed they didn't want to go to court over a couple of thousand pounds to feel humiliated and taken for a sucker. In truth, I wouldn't want to go to court and stand opposite him and his wife over a couple of grand. That is probably not what many people want to hear. The ending should show justice served and the women took the knobby man down – blah blah.

What came as a surprise was how the investigation revealed many of the women were having affairs too – they didn't want their long-term partners to find out they had given their lover money. That was the unfortunate reality rather than the romanticised ideal.

At this point in time I am grateful for Ryan, he was a catalyst. As much as he was a wombat he was a subtle driver to make me take time out to enjoy, rest and reflect. He would never have chosen to make such a trip and that is fine. It isn't for everyone but it was for me. I also have to say I am so glad my work gave me the opportunity. While I was away I actually missed work, I missed the satisfaction of the puzzles being unravelled. I gave myself a rest and realised that I liked my vocation.

I have since learned that I can make such a trip every couple of years. If I had not asked then it would not have been made available for everyone in the company. I doubt many will take the opportunity to go on such an adventure but it is now available for the brave and those who have savings.

Another thing I have decided for the next year is I will become a weekend wanderer. I do not need to travel far from home to recharge and feel like I have a holiday. I will take a rest from resting and once back into work I will make more time for adVANtures. If you have the chance then take it I say.

On a bit of a sombre note: Vanessa's friend died after six weeks of finding out she was terminal; however, she flew in a private jet, spent a week in a spa with her mother, did some race track days, made a parachute jump, flew in a gyrocopter and went scuba diving. She told Vanessa in the last six weeks of her life she had lived more and loved more than her previous forty years. She said to Vanessa the terrible realisation was that she had put off living for a future date because she assumed she would always have more time. She said she wished she had always made the most of her 'nows'. That truly resonated with me. Sometimes one really does have to say 'Stuff it!' because as much as I like paying my bills – there is more to life than that.

Oh dear... Back to work and...

On the day of my return to work – it was the quarter kick-off where there is a review of what has been achieved and they disclose the future strategy. I signed into the zoom call to see plenty of new faces and some well-worn looking old ones. The boss sat at the centre of the screen and saw me arrive. 'Welcome back!' He cried with a huge grin. 'How were the gnomes?'

CHAPTER 60

STUFF IT! REFLECTIONS

A bit of a reflection. I have to say it was a real pleasure to put this little book together because it enabled me time to indulge in what I experienced, the wonderful people I met and that it is well worth listening to one's intuition. I have to admit I did return to a bit of a work treadmill, where I was once again time poor and my life was ordered. So what I did was email myself each day a different part of the trip. I am so glad I did that now because I compiled this little beauty and realise how adVANture changed me and put things in perspective. Don't you find it strange how we have to justify being able to take time out? Why can't we just say 'Stuff it!' because we simply want to… Is there a better way? The trickiness comes in maintaining an income for adVANTtures. If one can have passive incomes or build a huge 'Stuff it!' fund then there is endless opportunity. If not, then it is a case of 'where there is a will there is a way!' If your heart and intuition say 'Stuff it!' then it is completely up to you to follow the call or do mini-regular 'Stuff its!' Remember you don't have to throw in the towel or make a spectacle of it. Plus a 'Stuff it!' does not have to be expensive. There are always ways and means.

With that in mind, if you have reached this part of the book, thank you. If you like it then please review and recommend it. I hope this will be a catalyst for others to have wonderful memories and recount their van/camping stories.

Love RUBY

NOT REALLY THE END

OTHER BOOKS IN THE SERIES:

STUFF IT! – VANDERLUST

OTHER SIMILAR BOOKS BY RUBY ALLURE

CRUISE SHIP CREATURES

Printed in Dunstable, United Kingdom